Life Coach Manual

First Responder Tools

Volume One

Dr. Rondall L. Bailes, DCH

Life Coach Manual

First Responder Tools

Volume One

All Rights Reserved © 2015 by Dr. Rondall L. Bailes, DCH

First Edition

No part of this publication may be reproduced, stored in any retrieval system, or transmitted, in any form or by any means, graphic or mechanical, including photocopying, recording, or otherwise be copied for public or private use-other than for "fair use" as brief quotations embodied in articles and reviews, without prior written permission of the author.

The author of this book does not give or dispense medical advice of any kind or prescribe directly or indirectly the use of any techniques as a form of treatment for any physical ailments, emotional issues or medical problems. The intent of the author is to offer information of a general nature to assist individuals on their journey to self-discovery and their quest for emotional and spiritual well-being. Should you use any information in this book for yourself, the author and publisher assume no responsibility for your actions.

Published by:
Ron Bailes International, Inc.
585 Hotel Plaza
Boulder City, Nevada 89005

For information
www.peoplereadingbodylanguage.com

Cataloging-in-Publication data for this book is available from the Library of Congress.

ISBN – 978-0-9845744-1-4

Dedication

This book is dedicated to all of the individuals studying to become a Life Coach and to those who are working to better their Life Coaching skills. I am proud to share many of the tools that I have used and/or developed over the years of my career as a Hypnotherapist and Life Coach. This book is also dedicated to everyone brave enough to embark upon the journey into self and take the necessary steps in changing their life for the better. My hope is the tools presented in this manual will help guide the way.

Acknowledgements

I sincerely give thanks to the following individuals that I am proud to call my friends for graciously sharing their time, opinions and expertise as they proofread this manuscript.

To Jeanette Markowski, I do recognize you have always worked tirelessly to finish every project and meet deadlines. Your input, keen eye for detail and opinions on the topics and subjects outlined in this book are truly valued. I would also like to take this opportunity to thank you for being willing at a moment's notice to drop what you are doing and put my projects first. Thank you, it is truly appreciated.

A very special thank you to Robyn Radig for all the projects you have worked on with me in the past and the ones we are working on currently. I appreciate you sharing your knowledge and interest in hypnosis as well as your time as I strived to refine many of the tools discussed in this book. I sincerely appreciate your eagerness, curiosity and understanding.

To Christine DeBuff I extend my deepest and sincere appreciation for rescuing me countless times by helping me with the baffling computer problems I encountered while writing this manual. I thank you for the countless hours you gave graciously on this project and for your enthusiasm and patience as you assisted me in the editing and preparation of this book for publication. Thank you!

To Lynn Perkins, once again I have called upon you to share with me your knowledge and talent. I appreciate your candid remarks and written comments while editing this manuscript. Thank you for sharing your expertise with me. I truly value your readiness to share your time and help me with my writing endeavors.

Again I give a special thank you to Myles B. 'Tim' Timmins, BCH. CI. OB my friend and colleague and chairman of the Las Vegas Chapter of The National Guild of Hypnotists for sharing your time, expertise and knowledge on the subjects and topics written about in this manual. I also thank you for taking the time to write the forward.

To Layne C. Keck, CHT, I am proud to have you as a friend and colleague. The discussions we have during our meetings of the Las Vegas Chapter of The National Guild of Hypnotists, where we gather with other likeminded individuals to share ideas and techniques is very insightful and thought provoking. As the director of the only qualified School of Hypnotism in Nevada, Capstone

Hypnotherapy I sincerely want to thank you for your expertise and giving your opinion about the contents of this manual.

To Dan DeBuff, again I am honored that you have shown interest in my writings and your enthusiasm to share your insights. Your eagerness to ask questions and discuss different aspects of this manuscript was truly my pleasure. I just want you to know that I appreciate your willingness to take the time and share with me your thoughts and interpretation of the contents of this manual.

A very special thanks to Clifford Weathers for sharing his IT skills and for keeping my network and computers up and running at a moment's notice, allowing us to keep the publication of this book on schedule.

To Ralph Leue', a great graphic artist, I thank you for saving me days of struggle by helping me with the graphics on the cover of this manual. Your willingness to share with me your eye for detail and knowledge is truly appreciated. I enjoyed working with you and creating my vision with your assistance.

Forward

Dr. Ron Bailes's new and exciting book, Life Coach Manual Volume One is a must have for anyone interested in the business of Consulting Hypnosis or Life Coaching. This book has been needed in the hypnosis business for a long, long time.

This book instructs how to start, how to do it and how to proceed as well as what tools to use for effective therapy. It is a comprehensive "How To Do It Book" for the beginning and seasoned Hypnotist/Life Coach looking to venture into a deeper level of understanding of themselves and their clients.

Dr.Ron lays out the step-by-step process, in detail, on the tools to assist the Hypnotist/Life Coach in developing the appropriate approach to achieve their desired outcome and helping the client achieve their goals and potential.

I have known Dr. Ron Bailes for several years and found his techniques to be very informative and useful. His book will enlighten the seasoned Hypnotist and Life Coach as well as shine the light for the beginner. His willingness to share his in-depth knowledge of the workings of the subconscious and how it pertains to making life changes is invaluable.

On behalf of myself and any and all other Hypnotists and Life Coaches using this book, I would like to thank Dr. Ron Bailes for his work in creating this manual.

Myles B. 'Tim' Timmins, BCH. CI. OB

Forward

Dr. Ron Bailes and I have become good friends in the many years of spending time every month during our meeting of the National Guild of Hypnotists. Our meetings focus on continuing education, and discussing various approaches to guiding clients to achieve lasting success in their goals.

In our exchanges we have realized that we are comrades in our pursuit of searching out the subconscious blocks that stand in the way of our client's success as well as educating them in ways of reframing the roles and patterns that they can take with them when they leave our sessions.

I am extremely impressed with Ron's ability to "touch all the bases" with his clear and accurate mapping of the "Tools" needed by the Life Coach to assist the client in unraveling and confronting the fears that have kept their goals out of reach.

Ron uses superb illustrations, metaphors and a great technique of Honoring the Voice, just to name a few of the tools that impressed me and have brought to me a better understanding that I may share with my clients.

The Life Coach Manual, First Responder Tools, is so invaluable in my estimation, that once published, it will be required reading for my students in a Nevada State Post Secondary Education approved course that I teach. I feel this book will provide my students with powerful tools in their studies as well as a continuing guide for their future clients.

Layne Keck, CHT
Director of Capstone Hypnotherapy
Las Vegas, Nevada

Introduction

This Life Coach Manual is about some of the many different processes and techniques that I have learned, developed, and used over the years. I consider them my "Tools." This manual is about those tools the Life Coach can use to assist clients in achieving a deeper understanding of themselves and making the appropriate changes in their life for which they are seeking your help.

This manual is also designed for those who are interested in helping others, as well as themselves. Using the tools, examples, and scripts in this manual will help the Life Coach assist the clients in making changes in certain chosen beliefs and behaviors, and will also facilitate the individual with discovering what needs to be changed so balance can become the norm in his life. The tools in this manual will help the Life Coach construct an environment of learning where the client can feel safe as he explores past traumas and/or negative circumstances in his life and reframes their meaning.

When the tools in this manual are used in conjunction with one another, they can help the Life Coach create an experience with the client where he can reframe and learn from what he may have perceived as past negative experiences. These past experiences are then viewed as a learning tool for preparation of what is to come in the future.

Many of those past experiences have left individuals seeking relief from emotional pain which they have endured since childhood. They may be unaware the unwanted behaviors they exhibit today are connected to those past negative experiences. Once they embark upon their journey into self, connections and corrections will take place on a subconscious level and be experienced in their thoughts and behaviors.

I have been involved in Life Coaching and have used hypnosis since the 1970s. Over the years I have been asked, "How do you know where to start or what analogies or illustrations to use first that will help someone make changes in their life?" My answer is simple? I listen to the client and make a determination based on what he reveals.

I have been told by my clients time and time again the examples I write on the board helps them to understand what has taken place and how to change the negative programming. Being a Life Coach or a combination Life Coach/Hypnotist and using hypnosis is one thing; giving the client tools to make changes is something entirely different.

This book has sprung from well over thirty years of experience working, studying, doing hypnosis, and being a Life Coach. During this time, I developed tools and processes to be used when working with fears, phobias, anger management, relationship issues, pre- and post-surgery, and low to no self-esteem, just to mention a few. By following the simple guidelines and examples laid out in this manual, it will help the Life Coach create new processes that are more effective. Don't be afraid to let yourself be creative.

Table of Contents

The Filter 1
Levels of Meaning 5
The Perceptual Defense Mechanism 13
    Denial 14
    Fantasy Formation 16
    Interjection 18
    Isolation 22
    Projection 27
    Regression 29
    Repression 31
    Sublimation 41
Reframing 47
    The First Reframing Question is: 51
    The Second Reframing Question is: 52
    The Third Reframing Question is: 53
    The Tree Metaphor 56
Trans-Actual Analysis 73
    Trans-Actual Analysis - Parent, Adult, Child 73
    The Parent 74
    The Adult 78
    The Child 80
Sources of Stress 83
    Progressive Accumulating Stress 85
    Anticipated Events 87
    Unexpected Events 88
    Personal Trait Stress 89
        Self-Imposed Perfectionism 93
        The Perfectionist 94
        Insecurity 95
Positive Attainment 99
    Denial – Anger – Action 99

- Denial 104
- Anger 110
- Action 112
- Control Dramas 115
  - The Quest for Power 115
  - Intimidator – Interrogator – Aloof – Poor Me 115
  - Intimidator 119
  - Interrogator 125
  - Aloof 127
  - Poor Me 129
- Behavior Patterns 133
  - Life – You – Stuff – Self Esteem 133
- Control / Approval 141
- Self-Esteem 153
  - Trust 155
  - Honesty 156
  - Responsibility 156
  - Integrity 157
  - Inner Voice 159
  - Emotions 161
  - Never Hurt Self or Others 161
  - Hypnosis script 163
- Purpose 173
  - Consistency of Purpose 176
- Motivation and Focus 179
  - Meditation 187
- Own the Problem 193
  - Metaphor 194
  - Can you sell it? 198
  - Could you make a loan against it for repairs? 199
  - Can you junk the car? 199
- Life Cycles 203
- Asset List 215
  - Hypnosis Script 225
- Voice 233
- Ten-Year Plan 249
- Public, Private, Secret Self 263
- Mind Levels 267

Life Coach Manual

First Responder Tools

Volume One

The Filter

Often I'm asked, when you have a new or existing client how do you know where to begin? How do you know what to say or do with someone? My response is, "Well one of the first things I suggest you do is listen, don't wait to talk, don't try to show off all your techniques and knowledge, listen. Listen through your knowledge base."

Just like your home air conditioner has a filter made of a particular type of material to filter out the dust and dirt before it enters the air conditioner. The same goes for the oil filter on your car which filters out the impurities from the motor. You must be like a Filter as you listen to your clients.

Your Filter is made of your knowledge and experience. Filtering out the client's inconsistencies, harmful thoughts, beliefs, and behaviors requires focus and attention to

"Purpose" in order to help the client achieve his desired outcome.
(Refer to Purpose)

Ask questions that are relevant to their stated issue and really listen to what the person is saying. When you listen, listen on different levels. You can then begin to filter out the incongruences in the client's thoughts and beliefs. Many times he will state the problem and, when given the time, without realizing it, he will give the solution.
(Refer to Levels of Meaning)

The solution may be unacceptable to him consciously so he is unwilling to hear the answer. This is where you will help him to discover the answer using your tools, techniques, and metaphors. It is not our place as Life Coaches to give the answer, even though the client may have just said what needs to be done.

After the client and I have conversed for a while and he repeats a phrase over and over, many times I will interrupt and say, "Hold it just a minute, lets freeze frame what you just said." I then ask him, "Would you repeat that again in slow motion?"

Usually he will be unable to repeat what he had just said, so I will give him clues until he figures out what he has been saying. I then have him repeat it three or four times or until he hears and realizes what he has been subconsciously repeating to himself. This is where the light bulb goes on, the "Ah Hah" moment.

All information the client reveals is important and useful. To help the client realize his role in the problem, I explain, that I have categorized what he is saying into levels. This helps separate out the drama from the real issues. The client can be caught up in the drama to the extent he is unable to see beyond what is taking place, and how he is being affected mentally, physically, and emotionally.

Levels of Meaning

I use a whiteboard to display the tool that I am using at any particular time. Since I may refer back to something we have previously covered, I manage the space for more than one illustration. This allows the client's subconscious to continually absorb what is taking place. It also gives him a visual to refer back to as we move from one topic to the next.

I do not use the tools in any particular order. Where we will begin depends on the client and his issues. It's up to the Life Coach to determine where to start, what tools to use, and in what order. The key here is to possess enough tools to recognize where to start and how to proceed.

Levels of Meaning

    1 -   **Surface,** Drama

    2 -   He said, She said

    <u>3 -   They do this, They do that</u>

    4 -   **Physical,** Affects

    5 -   Anxiety, Depression,

    <u>6 -   Insomnia, Digestive problems</u>

    7 -   **Transition Level**

    <u>   Understanding comes /goes</u>

    8 -   **Meaning of Meaning**

    9 -   OR

    10 - **Spiritual Level**

This illustration is to give an example of the different levels an individual may be expressing his dilemma. It is also to help the Life Coach develop listening skills so he can assist the client in reaching a deeper level of understanding.

When using the Levels of Meaning tool, I proceed as follows:

After listening to my client for a while and when I think it is appropriate, I begin explaining the Levels of Meaning. I will write the numbers one through ten on the board. I then draw a line under number three and to the side I write "Surface Stuff."

I then draw a line under the number six, and to the side I write the words "Physical Stuff." Under number seven I draw a line, and to the side I write the word "Transition." Then to the side of eight, nine and ten, I write the words "Meaning of Meaning" or "Spiritual."

When he begins with "He Said, She Said" and/or "They Do This, They Do That," I put this drama next to the Surface numbers one, two and three. I then say, "They have the right to do, think, and act as they please. You have the right not to tolerate their remarks and actions."

The same process goes for the numbers, four, five and six in the Physical category. Woven into what the client is saying will be how he is being physically affected by what is going on or taking place in his life. This stress can result in a variety of behaviors: anxiety, depression, loss of sleep, stomach problems, just to mention a few.

The number seven I use as a Transition. This area is used when he seems to come to a realization, but then becomes confused about how to act upon the information. He just kind of understood. It is much like in school when the teacher is explaining something and you think you have it but then it's quickly gone.

I let him know I am listening and responding to him on a deep level. And I am listening for his solutions that are coming from his subconscious which he may consciously not want to accept until now. As he reveals these solutions woven into the fabric of his thoughts, I will write them next to the numbers eight, nine, and ten.

The following are brief explanations of the Levels of Meaning:

To become more effective, the Life Coach must develop the listening skill to separate inconsistencies of what is taking place between the levels. He must also identify and explain what is taking place on each level.

Levels 1-3
Surface Stuff, Drama, the more "Public You"
Many people attempt to live their lives on this level thus causing many problems. They will seem very shallow and

seldom connect problems in their life with their behaviors and beliefs. They seem to be oblivious of a deeper self.

Levels 4-6

Physical Stuff, the more "Private You"

Many people are afraid of this level or may not be consciously aware it exists because of feelings of failure, not good enough, past or present emotional pain, fear of loss, or abandonment, etc.

Level 7

Transitional level

Here is where people are beginning to understand or become aware of a deeper self. They will have a tendency to vacillate back and forth between their old way of thinking and the new way they are learning.

Level 8-10

More Spiritual level, also called the "Meaning of Meaning," a "Deeper You"

Thinking on these levels aligns the other levels in a more cohesive thought process. A more balanced person emerges from an old thought process which has been keeping the individual from achieving the desired outcome in their life.

Here is the purpose of this tool/exercise. It is to help the person realize the incongruences of what is being said and how he is not hearing what he is saying on a deep spiritual level. By listing key phrases next to the different numbers, the client begins to visually see how he is at odds with himself.

This exercise also demonstrates how he may actually be hiding from a truth or a particular course of action that needs to be taken to resolve the issue. By staying distracted and involved in the drama and the emotional pain, he may be consciously unaware of how it is affecting him physically.

The process helps the client to differentiate between the surface drama of a situation and the physical aspects as well as the deeper meaning of what he is experiencing. By understanding what he needs to learn from this experience, he will gain insight into his role in the situation. This will assist him in gaining the ability to make decisions in his best interests.

As we carefully listen to people, they will reveal their problem and the solution; they are just unable to hear the solutions themselves. I simply began listening for their solutions on a deep level. I am truly listening and not waiting to talk.

(Refer to Reframing and Control/Approval)

The Perceptual Defense Mechanism

The Perceptual Defense Mechanism is typically one of the first tools I use. I use this tool like filters as I listen to my client tell about his situation. The tool has several components and will help you to determine which other tools to use. It will also give insight into the direction the session will take.

I may not necessarily inform the client that I am using this tool or any other, but will simply listen to him and keep the components of the tool in the forefront of my mind. I use them as filters to determine what issues I will approach first or take on next.

As I think it is necessary, I will explain the components and will write them on the whiteboard so my client will actually have a visual. The information will be left on the board in front of him during the entire session so his subconscious is continually exposed to each component. As mentioned above, I may simply be using it as a listening filter.

Denial

Denial is the first component I listen for, even though I will be aware of others during the same time. There are several ways that people can deal with denial. Through projection they project fault or blame onto another individual. They may just flat deny any involvement or their role in a given situation. Many times, it is because they can't face their responsibility, or lack of, or they may not be able to handle the truth.

A woman I was working with told me that she had made contact with her children's father. She wanted the children, now in their 20s, to visit and build a relationship with their father. The visit did not go so well.

The father had a whole different perception of what it was like when they were young and had these babies. His recollection was when they were separated he got up every morning or pretty regularly went to McDonald's and bought breakfast and took it to the children at the wife's house. He also stated he went to McDonald's regularly and bought lunches, and he also regularly walked the children to school.

Her perception as she told the story was totally different. As the confrontation between the two of them escalated, she said to him, "I don't know whose children you were taking that food to but it wasn't my kids. You must have been hallucinating."

"You never brought them McDonald's, you never walked them to school nor did you ever pay child support. You made them promises to pick them up and take them places, but you never showed up even though they were watching and waiting for hours."

He blamed her for poisoning the kids' minds against him and for taking the children away from him. He asked her, "Did you tell them that when we had these babies I was young and immature. I never paid child support because things were tough and the list goes on."

In his mind, he had conjured up an experience that was acceptable and possibly what he wanted. However, being in denial helped him from dealing with feelings of guilt or feeling irresponsible. I usually tell my clients that denial can be a wonderful thing: "It's also a river in Egypt."

Fantasy Formation

Fantasy Formation is one of the next components the Life Coach will want to listen for during the conversation. Here is where an individual perceives reality out of some fantasy. Their life motives are unsatisfied in the objective world, so they handle this fantasy formation through entertainment. They find adventure, security, and even affection through their fantasies.

Basically, what I'm saying here is through entertainment they get their adventure rather than go on an adventure. The same goes for affection and security. Rather than risk being hurt or rejected or taking the chance of something going wrong, they will fantasize what it would be like to have that experience. In this fantasy they can live out and control what is not otherwise vividly expressed in their objective life.

Fantasy Formation is a major player in the Defense Mechanism. As a Life Coach it is very important to be aware of and to utilize this component. When you really start connecting the dots, you'll find in many cases your client will be operating someplace within these different components, if not in several.

I had a client bring his fiancée to see me to help them with some relationship issues. They were both in their mid-forties. He was an executive for a large company and she was employed by a contractor who did work for that company. He was very business-minded, needless to say. She on the other hand was a party animal, of which he was to find out later.

She liked to go clubbing on the Las Vegas Strip three or four nights a week. He was to find this out later after the relationship had become more serious. He was more straight-laced and didn't drink or smoke, do drugs, or hang out at the casinos. He soon found out she did all of the above, and then some. It's easy to see why they had problems.

During a session with her, she revealed that many times she would get so wasted that she would have no idea at which casino she parked her car. She said there were many occasions she would wake up in some strange man's bed the next day and have no idea how she got there or what had taken place.

She also stated she had been missing a lot of work and had been showing up late almost every day. It wasn't long until she was fired. She continued to party, spend money she didn't have, and overdraw her bank account. He would cover her overdrafts but was tired of it and something had to change.

I asked her to help me to understand why a woman in her forties would behave that way. She replied that at her age she should be able to have fun and that it was nobody's business what she does. She also said she liked to dress up and go to the clubs and "pretend" to be a Rock Star.

This is what I mean by fantasy formation. You don't have to be a couch potato, watch national geographic, and fantasize. You may pretend you are somebody you're not by playing a role and living beyond your means. The fantasies of entitlement may allow for certain behaviors at a particular age that may not otherwise be experienced in one's objective life.

Interjection

Interjection is the next defense mechanism component we will explore. Interjection helps defend against disappointment and disillusionment. In this component, the Life Coach will be listening for the way individuals blame themselves for whatever has taken place in their life, even as far back as early childhood.

For example, a child feels unworthy of the parents attention because the parents' do not give attention to the child. Or, when the child was very young he did not receive the affection he needed from his parents. Now, as an adult, he may have deep feelings of being unworthy.

You will want to give close attention to this component as the client is telling you of his issues. This is especially true when he is having relationship problems, personally as well as professionally, and is taking all of the blame when it is clearly the fault of another.

Of course, there is something for him to learn from this situation. If there wasn't something for him to learn, he would not be experiencing the emotional pain of which he is speaking. In order for me to help him, this is the component that becomes my point of focus.

Recently a woman in her early thirties came to see me because her husband was constantly berating her, and hitting her. He would not come home for three or four days at a time, with no communication, no phone call, and no explanation. His comments were, "I don't answer or explain myself to anyone."

As she spoke, I listened. I would ask general questions from time to time to help her reveal what she was going through. She said they had been married a little over a year, they did not have children, and this behavior began within a few months after the wedding.

She whispered, "I can't figure out what I'm doing wrong things just keep getting worse." As I began to ask more pointed questions, she began to make excuses for him. "I want him to get help because I think he is bipolar."

When I addressed the hitting issue she told me, "He doesn't hit me all of the time, only when I do something wrong or when he gets really angry. I don't think it's his fault because he had a bad childhood. I don't think he can help it, that's why I think he must be bipolar or something."

When I asked about him disappearing for days, her reply was, "I don't think he remembers. At least that's what he said when I threatened to leave. Then things would be okay for a few days or a week then it starts all over again."

As she sat there crying, I said, "So you have thought about leaving." She replied, "Yes, but I don't want to, I love him. And besides, then everyone would know I screwed up again." She went on to say, "At least when things are good he gives me attention and affection, and that's more than I ever got from anyone else."

At this point I began asking questions and discussing her childhood. Here is where she revealed that she is the black sheep of the family and could never do anything right. She said everyone pretty much ignored her and never paid attention to anything she had to say. "Now all I need is to get divorced."

Here is a perfect example of Interjection, unresolved childhood issues continuing to create major issues in the adult. It may be true that she doesn't know how to choose a man. It also may be true that this is a self-esteem issue.

Her current issues can be used as the doorway to a life-changing event. She can learn to reframe the past, find the positive, take charge of her life, and possibly hone her skills in choosing a partner. To help her, I started with the tools Denial, Anger, Action and then the Steps to Self-Esteem.

Isolation

Isolation is our next component. It is the avoidance of connecting associations related to ideas that produce any amount of anxiety. A few examples would be birth from death, war from mourning, nuclear arsenals from murderous horror. As we think about it, these may be obvious and for good reason.

Many times we isolate different behaviors and thought processes from a particular outcome because the results may not match our desires, so we ignore the facts and "think positive" (hope for the best). Making decisions based on facts, in most cases, brings about positive results.

When my client is telling me about what he is experiencing, I am listening for the way he isolates what is going on in his life from the way he thinks and what he has

come to believe. This is another example of why I use the whiteboard to show visual illustrations.
(Refer to Levels of Meaning)

Using the isolation component as a tool, connections will need to be made. For example, when working with relationship issues, I would begin connecting the devastation this breakup will have on the family, with their children being first and foremost.

Even though they may already know all of this on a subconscious level, we are simply using the isolation component to bring as many factors as possible to a conscious level. Together we work to help them reconnect and take a snapshot of the big picture. We then break the issues down to find what caused the changes that have taken place.

We work together connecting what brought them together in the first place. We also explore how they got to where they are now. Connections are then made as to why they were married or became life partners. All of these connections are then attached to when the problems began and how they escalated. The objective here is to have them

realize there are many options when repairing a relationship.
(Refer to Reframing and Owning the Problem)

For example, on the whiteboard I may explain the tools, Denial, Anger, Action. Then I will ask each one of them to talk for twenty minutes about their perception of what it was like when they met and when times were good and to then talk about when things started going bad and how they got so ugly.

I call this talk the good, the bad, the ugly. The one that is listening cannot interrupt, nor are they allowed to defend themselves when it's their turn to talk. They simply tell their perception of the good, bad, ugly. I have found this process is a very good way to begin making connections.

One of the most common issues is that neither of them feels they are listened to or "heard." Each of them is caught up in defending themselves with every statement made by the other. This twenty-minute uninterrupted talk can do wonders by letting them say their peace. Sometimes a relationship has run its course and there is no saving it, especially when one of them is done and just wants out. *(Refer to Denial, Anger, Action)*

Some time back, a woman in her forties came in to see me about problems she was having at work. She said that some of her co-workers were being rude and short with her and she was being completely ignored by others. With a baffled look on her face she said she had no idea why this was happening.

I asked her, "So tell me a little about what is going on in your life these days." She replied, "Not much. About all I do is work, which I like, but lately that has been miserable too." So I asked, "What do you mean by 'that has been miserable too?' What else is causing you misery?"

She then began to tell how her home life had not been so great. She and her boyfriend had been fighting a lot, she is unhappy, so everything seems to be a struggle. She wasn't getting much sleep because of all the arguing.

I asked her, "In what way do you think your home life may be affecting your work life? Are you showing up for work on time? Have you been cheery and friendly at work during this time of trouble at home?"

She replied that she has been getting to work on time but cannot help from crying off and on throughout the day. She also said it is very hard to focus and that she has been keeping to herself as much as possible. She also stated, "No, I have not been very cheery and friendly. It's hard to be that way when I'm so unhappy."

I then explained that we have a public self, a private self, and a secret self. After we discussed the role of each, I told her she has been taking her private self to work, which is only a place for her public self. Her co-workers only need to know her public self.

I further explained she can't be expressing her private mood swings at your place of employment without making others uncomfortable. Everyone has to deal with their own personal issues. They are not at work to take on others personal problems.

She quickly replied, "I HAVE A RIGHT TO MY FEELINGS AND EMOTIONS, DON'T I?" I said to her,

"You certainly do and the problems you are having at work are the fallout from expressing them in the wrong environment." I also told her she has many rights that may not necessarily serve her best interests.

She had no idea "her" attitude and behavior were connected to her workplace problems. She felt "her" behavior was justified because of her emotional pain. She thought everyone should show a little understanding and compassion. This is an excellent example of isolation. *(Refer to Public, Private, Secret Self)*

Projection

I always pay close attention to this component, keeping in mind there are always two sides to every story. Projection is much like denial. When anything happens, the person just projects it onto another person or to another incident. They blame the government, they blame school, they blame the teacher, and they blame the police when they get a ticket. Nothing is ever their fault; they project anything and everything onto another person or object.

Because they lack the skills it takes to learn from their mistakes, they project. This defends them against dealing with something they don't know how to handle. My experience has been that Projection has its beginnings in childhood and is then reinforced throughout the years.

A few years ago when the seatbelt law went into effect, my friend's wife got a citation for not wearing her seatbelt. She had been driving his car for a couple of weeks while hers was in the repair shop. The seatbelt latch was broken in his car and would not buckle. The problem is she didn't get the ticket in his car she got it in her car.

About three weeks after she got her car out of the shop she was pulled over for not wearing her seatbelt and received a citation. She came home and gave the ticket to her husband and said, "You got a ticket today for me not wearing my seatbelt."

He said, "What are you talking about woman?" She said that she got out of the habit of wearing the seatbelt while driving his car and so it was his fault she got the ticket. Even though the story is lighthearted, it is a good example of Projection.
(Refer to Reframing)

Regression

Regression is common in a serious illness or major trauma. Here is where the individual regresses back to an earlier stage of development, when someone else assumes responsibility for the person. It will be a time when they had fewer and simpler needs and more primitive goals. They live a basic existence as it is a concerted effort for them to get up and move around.

When working with someone who has entered this dark place, the Life Coach must be prepared to move very slowly. One of the tools I use is hypnosis for relaxation and post-hypnotic suggestions. While they are hypnotized, I will subtly begin reframing some of the issues that I uncovered during the pre-talk.

I do not take the main trauma head-on; it may be too painful for them. I will slowly work on reframing some of their less traumatic issues to get them comfortable with the process. As the client shows improvement, we will start chipping away and reframing what caused them to be in their current state of mind.

I will also do ego-strengthening, self-esteem, and self-confidence with them. I wait until they reach a time when they mention correcting a few bad habits, such as drinking or smoking or any other negative behavior. I simply consider those habits and behaviors their self-medication.

For instance, when they ask if I can use hypnosis to help them stop smoking or drinking, I answer, "Yes, but let's take them one at a time." I will explain how they possibly use these substances to cope with their emotional pain and advise them that we will work on one at a time and deal with the issues that arise.

The Life Coach will want to help the client find Purpose. Many times helping them make 'short' and long-term plans achieves this goal. Start with simple things for them to do, like writing a letter about their feelings to the other person, even if the other person has passed. You may have them write a poem about what has happened if they are the creative type.

The following is a short synopsis of what happened to a very close friend of mine and her family. My friend's younger sister was found murdered. Even though the family went to counseling they struggled for many years. My friend and her father and brother learned the necessary coping skills to continue on with their lives in spite of the emotional pain.

However, the mother did not fare so well and was unable to move forward in life. She went into a deep depression and began to regress back to a simpler time. Before this tragedy she was vibrant, full of energy, and quick-witted; afterwards she seldom left the house.

She spent her days watching television, smoking cigarettes, and drinking beer. Shortly after I met my friend, her father passed away and she moved back home to care for her then elderly mother. Here is an example of a traumatic experience that brought about the regression.

Repression

Repression acts like an invisible filter that censors or prohibits painful memories, associations, and adjustments from conscious awareness. It has a very broad range and can filter everything from cruelty to embarrassment. Even though this emotional pain may be blocked from conscious awareness it still has an effect on the person.

As I am working with a client, I listen for the undercurrent of pain that repression may cause in his life. This undercurrent can show up in the person's life as fears, phobias, and/or negative behaviors. These behaviors may seem normal to him because he doesn't connect them with any particular incident. However, at any time, something can trigger that incident and it can become conscious.

Not long ago, I received a phone call from a former client who asked if he could get an appointment as soon as possible. He told me something had happened and he needed my help. He said he had no one he could talk with about it, not even his wife.

He is a successful businessman, about fifty years old. When he arrived for his appointment, he told me that he has property in Arizona where he and his wife are going to build a home and retire. He said that he already built a metal building/shop where he has been moving tools and other items.

He said normally they travel back and forth together, but this time his wife had other appointments so he decided to go alone. It had been a few months since they had been there and he needed to check on the place. He was going to tow their travel trailer down and leave it so they would have a place to stay while they were there working.

When he arrived he found the place had been broken into. Someone had cut a hole in the metal building and had taken everything of value. He said, talking about feeling violated, "I was completely caught off guard. By the time the police arrived and took their report it was getting late in the day."

Even though he was very tired, he decided to drive back home that night. After driving for a couple of hours he had a flashback to his childhood that scared the wits out of him. It made him so nervous he had to pull off the road and try to regain his composure. Since then, he had not been able to get it out of his mind.

He stated that all of a sudden he remembered his stepfather molesting him when he was seven. He said, "I remembered what I was wearing, exactly where it took place, what he did, the smell of his breath, all in vivid detail. I don't know what to do with this. I've been unable to focus. I can't get it out of my mind. I don't keep secrets from my wife, but how do I tell her something like this about me?"

He went on to say, "I can see why I got away with so many things as a child and teenager." He said he never remembered being alone with his stepfather again; his mother was always there on all of their outings. He further said, "Even though she was deathly afraid of boats she would still go with us. I remember being alone with my Mom but not him. As a child, I never put any of this together and never connected the dots."

With a great sense of urgency in his voice he asked, "What am I going to do with this, how am I going to be able to deal with this, what I am going to tell my wife? Why haven't I remembered this before now?" I mainly sat and listened, saying very little, so he could "get it all out."

I finally responded to him and said, "We have to reframe the entire experience. What I mean by 'reframe' is you have to change the meaning of what has happened. It's not going to be easy at first, nor will it be a quick fix. In order for you to heal and put this behind you, we must be thorough."

I told him many times as children we block out traumatic experiences which we are unable to process. To reinforce our rapport and to give him hope, I told him how I had reframed some very negative childhood experiences using certain techniques and processes.

I then asked him to tell me the positive side of his experience, now that he had told me the negative. He gave me a puzzled stare and said, "What do you mean, tell you the positive side. There is no positive side." I explained that everything has two sides: up/down, round/square, in/out, positive/negative. I asked him again to tell me the positive.

Since he knew about equipment and machinery, I explained that if he would take the positive battery cable off his truck it will not start. The same goes for the negative cable. It needs both the positive and the negative cables connected to the battery for the truck to start. I then asked if he agreed. He replied, "I agree."

I immediately told him that the same goes for life experiences. However, it seems we have a natural tendency to only focus on the negative. We must train ourselves to seek out the positive, especially during times of emotional pain like what he is experiencing.

I told my client that my stepfather had taken my childhood, but I would not give him my adulthood. I would not let him put into my mind and spirit his anger, rage, and ignorance. I did not have a choice back then, but I do now. However, I had to learn how to reframe what had happened to me.

I began explaining to him the process and how the "Reframing Tool" helped me to understand, so I would be able to forgive and heal. I told him that he has the right to be angry about what has happened, however, he also has the right not to be angry. I explained that anger is an active emotion and will eat its way out of him either through an illness and/or some negative behavior.

I then asked him how he would feel if he caught a man scratching his new truck with a key. To put it nicely, he said, he would be very angry. I further asked him how he would feel if the man was obviously mentally challenged.

Would you still be angry at him or would you be angry at the incident? The reply was: "angry at the incident." In a lighthearted way, I said that if it were me, I would start looking for the person responsible for him so I could direct my anger toward him. But then, our point here is to get rid of anger.

Once we established that he would no longer be angry at the man, the level of anger is greatly diminished. I then explained this is how I began to view my stepfather. I asked myself, "How could anyone in their right mind abuse a child." My answer was, "They could not."

Although I didn't know or understand my stepfather's mental condition back then, I came to realize he did not have all of his "wires" plugged into the right place. It was true he could go to work, feed himself, drive, and do things that we would consider as normal, but that doesn't change the fact that he was still screwed up in the head.

After quite sometime of trying to understand the problem, I managed to direct my energy away from my stepfather and onto the incidents. I then asked myself, "Why did these things happen to me?" There had to be a reason. Maybe I was supposed to learn something from the way I had been treated. After awhile, I realized that I had embarked upon a journey to take back my life by changing negative thoughts and feelings into positives ones.

My client and I then began to go through the Reframing process together, working with his issue of molestation. It can be very difficult to come up with positives the first few times someone goes through the process. I will make suggestions based on what he has revealed about himself and some of his positive attributes.

To help him with finding answers when he was stuck, I shared with him some of what I had found about myself as I went through the process or what he had revealed earlier about himself. For example: independent, determined, self-starter, self-motivator, confident, take-charge attitude, not one that quickly jumps to conclusions, etc.

After we went through the Reframing process, I reminded him of our objective. It is to get rid of his emotional pain and the anger of the betrayal. I asked him if he was feeling better. He said, "Surprisingly, yes, I do feel better. I certainly have a different perspective and I'm not hurting like I was earlier."

I then explained to him that there is another very important part to releasing the pain and the anger of what he is experiencing. This next step involves some critical thinking and a bit of soul-searching. Hopefully, during this next step, he will find forgiveness in his heart. He responded by saying, "I don't think that will ever happen."

I asked if I gave him a home work assignment would he do it and he said "yes." So I suggested he write a letter to his stepfather. I call the letter "the good, the bad, and the ugly." In the letter I told him to say what he thinks, how he feels, and how he was affected by his stepfather's actions.

He said that his stepfather had passed away a few years ago, so it wouldn't do any good to write him a letter, but if he were still alive he would "kick his butt." I told him it doesn't matter and to write the letter anyway, it is not about his stepfather, but rather about his own healing process.

He returned the next week with letter in hand. The letter contained some very explicit language as the client expressed his feelings. He then said that about halfway through the letter he actually began to feel sorry for his stepfather. He said he realized his stepfather was a very sick man.

My client said he began to realize what torment his stepfather must have gone through the rest of his life, always wondering when he would blurt out what his stepfather had done to him. He said this explains a lot about why he got away with the things he did as a teenager.

He had let his wife read the letter and said he felt good about sharing it with her and what had happened. He also revealed that he wanted to confront his elderly mother about what had taken place, but his wife disagreed with him about contacting his mother.

I, too, disagreed with confronting his mother. I told him that bringing such pain to her would serve no purpose. Based on what he had told me, his mother had done the best she could with what she knew. During the time when all of this had taken place there were no women's shelters or any of the services available today.

I told him we are not here to fix his stepfather or his mother; we are here to help him stop his pain. The only way he can change what happened in the past, is to reframe and change what it means to him. The objective is to find how it made him a better person.

I said to him that after the letter is written and all has been said, bring the letter to his next session and read it to me, so if something of importance has been left out, I can ask him questions and he can put the answers into the letter. I then suggested he burn the letter to symbolically let go of his anger and pain. This is the process that worked for me and for others that I have helped.
(Refer to Reframing)

Sublimation

Sublimation is a redirection drive mechanism; it's a substitution of a primitive sense for a more socially acceptable behavior. This redirecting of unacceptable impulses, especially sexual desires, can be experienced in more socially acceptable creative activities.

This acceptable behavior can be seen in the way we take out our primal impulses and aggression in sports. For instance, football, volleyball, boxing, or any other sport that is an acceptable behavior may redirect those energies to become more socially accepted.

The Life Coach will want to listen very closely and give special attention to this particular component. Often clients come to me with issues of feeling empty, sad, and depressed. They tell me how busy they are, they tell of their volunteer work and other social activities, but they still feel unfulfilled.

Here is a good example of sublimation. Although the redirection mechanism is in place, those deep primitive drives are not being met. They are surfacing through other emotional symptoms. Rather than seek out those drives and deal with them, we have a tendency to treat the symptoms.

The approach I prefer taking is the one I used on my own personal journey. The process for discovering real issues are what I call a journey into self. I liken it to a corkscrew, where we slowly worm our way down into the subconscious to find what is missing in life which we may not be consciously aware of. This process involves being flexible and responding to those suppressed and repressed emotions as they surface.

These defense mechanisms are showing each of us only what we want to see about ourselves and the world around us. It requires a conscious effort to seek out, correct, and resolve those beliefs that limit our abilities and potential. We must go beyond ego-driven defenses.

Over the years many of my clients have made comments or asked questions about how they feel, as though it is about right or wrong or good or bad. Rather than accepting and embracing their true feelings and beliefs, they repress them for fear of being rejected. I will explain to them that before you can change a problem or behavior, you must own it, otherwise you remain stuck.
(Refer to Owning the Problem)

Acting appropriately in any given situation is much different then repressing and suppressing who you really are just to fit in with the "in crowd." When this occurs, it immediately becomes a self-esteem issue. As time goes by, behavior problems begin to develop as well as, I believe, illness. *(Refer to Self-Esteem)*

I explain to my clients it is not about what you are supposed to think or feel, but rather what you as an individual believe and feel. If these deep feelings and beliefs are bringing emotional pain, then they must be dealt with on the level on which they are being experienced. This process may require learning something new and/or reframing existing beliefs.

Many times the conscious mechanism is not a necessary part of the information processing system. The unconscious can, and quite frequently does, operate without, or at least unknown, to the conscious mechanism. On a conscious level you may not know why you are acting in a particular way.

We can have emotions, behaviors, and issues going on below our level of awareness. We may not be consciously aware that what is causing us problems, is taking place subconsciously. These emotions, behaviors, and issues often are seated in childhood and are the result of some type of abuse and/or misinformation. They may also be from other issues, as an adult, such as a breakup, betrayal or abuse.

Many beliefs are formed from misinformation when we were young. Even though these beliefs are incorrect they still may be carried into adulthood. As adults they can and do cause problems such as feelings of guilt, low self-esteem, lack of self-confidence, just to mention a few.

The subconscious mind is a "yes mind" and does not discern whether something is a truth or non-truth. When we are young our creative mind takes in bits and pieces of information and then, fills in the blanks. It then believes this misinformation to be fact and unless it is corrected immediately, it becomes a part of our Belief System.

We may obtain misinformation from parents, adults, teachers, clergy, friends, authority figures, or society in general. As we grow into adulthood we develop certain behaviors that we think are normal, even though they may be destructive to our well-being.

These components of the Defense Mechanism are tools which can give the Life Coach insight into the many facets of his client. Along with other tools and skills, they can be used to assist in getting to the root of issues which may be causing problems.

The Life Coach must develop active listening skills. This involves the ability to listen on many levels. The information must be processed through the filters of the many tools which the Life Coach has in his tool chest. Listening for what is not being said also can be a very valuable skill to possess.

At times it may be difficult to separate the facts from the drama in which the client may be involved. As you listen to an individual, keep in mind there are two sides to every story. Learn to listen on many levels. Part of the responsibility of a Life Coach is to help the client work through the drama. He also must assist the client in discovering and dealing with what is really going on deep within, which may be holding him back from his desires and full potential.

Reframing

Reframing is another one of my first responder tools when working with a variety of issues. It helps the client to realize there are two sides to every experience. I have found that most of the time people tend to focus on the negative and not even be aware of the positive side of what they have experienced or are currently experiencing.

It's as though we are programmed to go to the negative aspect of an experience rather than the positive. By shifting our attention to the positive, the experience then becomes a part of the learning process. When we view the experience as a learning process, it then becomes a positive in our life.

Taking control of your life, owning your situation, and taking action to make the changes can be very rewarding. The process it takes to bring peace and happiness into your life can be shrouded in excuses and fears. In most cases, these fears and excuses lie below our level of awareness and are a result of perceived past negative programming of either inferred or direct verbal or physical abuse.

These past experiences can leave an individual with low to no self-esteem and/or lack of confidence to believe he can take responsibility and make the changes necessary to make his life healthier. Even though some individuals recognize these fears and excuses exist, they still may not know how to go about making those changes.

One of the first steps the Life Coach must take in the process is to help the person take ownership of his issues. This is explained in the chapter "Own the Problem." This can be done by helping the client find what he wants from the situation or person involved. Their choices must be narrowed down to either "The Want of Control or The Want of Approval."
(Refer to Control/Approval)

Reframing is a very powerful tool that is used to make life changing decisions. These life-changing decisions come from the core of our identity. They come from the process of achieving a deep understanding of self and a desire to live a more fulfilling life despite what may have happened in one's life. It is the process of taking back one's power.

I have personally used the Reframing tool to change the direction of my life. When using the Reframing tool there is a shift that takes place in the way we think, feel, and respond to past negative experiences. This shift stems from a willingness to take charge of our life and release the hurt, anger, and the desire for revenge.

So many times my client has told me, "I have a right to be angry" or "They don't deserve to be forgiven." My response is, "It's not about them; it's about you. It's you who is being affected by what they did, not them. As long as you keep those feelings of hurt, anger, resentment, thoughts of revenge, and being violated inside, that person has power over you."

Reframing has to do with changing the meaning of those negative experiences which have taken place in the past or are possibly taking place in the present. Everything has two sides, a positive and a negative, even though it may not appear that way on the surface.

Sometimes it can be very difficult to find the positive in what seems to be a very negative experience. This is what Reframing is all about: thinking outside of the box and being in search of a better way. It actually liberates a person from the repressed and suppressed anger brought on by those negative experiences. This anger can cause a multitude of problems in one's life.

Before using this tool, the Life Coach must first establish and get an agreement with the client that there are two sides to everything. I ask my clients if they can think of anything on earth that only has one side; better yet, is there anything in the universe that only has one side. After a few moments of thought they reply that there is not. To establish it as fact, I respond with the following: "up/down, in/out, round/square, positive/negative."

I then repeat, "So everything has two sides: a positive and a negative. You have been telling about the negative you have experienced, so now tell me about the positives of that experience." This is a very important step in the Reframing process. It leaves the client no choice but to search for a positive to his negative experience.

When he states there is nothing positive about what had happened to him, and he will, I simply refer back that I thought we had established everything has a positive and a negative. Here is where a little help from the Life Coach may be necessary in the form of a few examples. The negative experience may have made him a hard worker, self-reliant, or a good parent.

The Reframing tool basically consists of three simple, yet deep, philosophical questions. To change a negative experience into a positive, one must contemplate each question with a sincere desire for positive personal growth and the willingness to forgive, even though it may not seem possible in the beginning.

The First Reframing Question is:

What positive did I learn about myself from what has happened to me? Or, what positive am I supposed to learn about myself from what I am now experiencing? As mentioned in the beginning, it may be difficult to find a positive, especially in a perceived negative experience.

It doesn't matter whether the experience was in the past or is happening in the present. Asking this question will immediately shift the thought process from a victim or defensive stance to an offensive or positive approach. In many cases, this first question will begin to neutralize feelings of guilt, anger, and resentment. In other words, whatever had happened in the past has now become part of a learning process.

The Second Reframing Question is:

How does this new positive information make me a better person? It may have made him a better parent, spouse, or friend. It may have made him have compassion, understanding, and forgiveness. It may have made him strong, independent, and motivated to make his life have a deeper meaning.

It's up to each individual to determine how both his positive and negative past experiences have made him a better person. This also includes problems he may presently be experiencing even though they may not seem to be any fault of his own. This process is not about fault; it's about personal growth.

The Third Reframing Question is:

How can I use this new positive information in my future to make my life better? Once you have discovered how past experiences, whether positive or negative, your fault or someone else's, can make your future better, then it's a matter of working on making adjustments in the way you think, feel, and behave.

With a new understanding and looking at past experiences as a learning tool in the process of becoming a better person, you simply stop blaming and making excuses. It is a matter of taking responsibility for your actions and learning something positive from all of your life experiences.

This process puts you more in control of your thoughts, feelings, and emotions. Your thoughts, feelings, and emotions affect your stress level which in turn, affects the muscles, organs, and tissues of your body. It's not very difficult to connect the effects of stress to health problems.

To assist the client in the Reframing process the Life Coach must keep in mind no matter the issue, whether physical or emotional, or mental abuse, abandonment, molestation, etc., there is a positive side to everything, even though at the time it may seem next to impossible to find.

The way the positive is found is by Reframing the experience. This, in most cases, will require a bit of coaching by the Life Coach, but not actually providing the client with the answers. It's up to the client to find his own positive answers.

The Life Coach only gives clues and asks questions to lead the client to the positive side of the experiences. An example question is as follows: "Why do you think 'nature' (*God, depending on their belief system*) put you in that situation to have that experience? It must have been for a good reason or it would not have happened."

The following metaphor is one I use in the Reframing process: This *metaphor* indirectly assists the client in realizing the experiences in his past can be used to make positive changes in his present and future. The storms the tree endured and the details of how growth took place symbolize the growth of his life and the roots of his identity. This metaphor indirectly assists the client in realizing the experiences in his past can be used to make positive changes in his present and future.

In the metaphor I have the client reflect back on his life and make comparisons between his experiences and the life and struggles of the tree. The client begins on a deep subconscious level to realize the challenges and struggles which he has gone through are natural and a mere learning experience for growth and change.

Keep in mind, the client's subconscious will be identifying with everything that is going on with the tree, including the root system, the new growth, and the healing. It is very important to paint a detailed image in the client's mind. When doing hypnosis I use scripts like this one to do what I call "Locking It In." The foregoing comes after explaining the Reframing exercise and many times doing waking hypnosis and using other appropriate tools for the situation.

The Tree Metaphor

Take a moment and relax. Just take a deep breath through your nose and hold it a few moments, now release the breath through your mouth. Now take another deep breath through your nose hold it a few moments and now release it through your mouth. Now take another deep breath through your nose, hold it, hold it, now release it through your mouth and just let your eyes go closed.

Now just begin to relax your eyes, relax the fronts of your eyes, relax the sides of your eyes, relax the backs of your eyes. Begin now to relax all of the tissue around your eyes. Let it become soft and pliable, easy and gentle, cool and comfortable, so relaxed that all of the muscles around your eyes, throughout your face, scalp, and neck just let go as you move deeper and deeper into a total and complete state of relaxation.

Relax your eyes just as though you were asleep now, relax your eyes just as though you (are) asleep now. Relax your eyes until they just won't work now, relax your eyes until they just won't work now. When you are absolutely sure they just won't work now, very gently test them.

Now let that relaxation fall down through your entire body. Let it move down into your chest; let it tumble down through your abdomen, relaxing everything in its path. Let it move down through your groin, down through your thighs, your knees, down through your calves, through your ankles, into your feet and right out the bottom of your feet.

Now, experience this relaxation throughout your entire body, through every muscle in your body, through every blood vessel in your body, through every nerve ending, all the way down to the bone marrow.

As you experience this relaxation taking place, let your mind begin to drift, let your thoughts begin to wonder about new ways, and new things and new attitudes, new behaviors. Let your mind begin to drift to other places. Imagine your thoughts beginning to wonder about what it would be like if you now take a new look at the way you think, at the way you feel, and the way you behave.

And you realize that it's now time to make changes, and you wonder about what those changes might be, what would be the benefits to you? What would be the benefits to you, if you now let your thoughts begin to shift, to change, to take on a new perspective?

And you just imagine with your mind drifting and your thoughts wondering about this new perspective. Imagine if you took some time, you took some time alone to do some thinking, to restructure, to prioritize, not only your life, but the way you think and the way you feel about life, and what you came here on this earth to do.

Imagine going for a walk in the forest, the trees are tall, the temperature is just right, the smell of the forest, the path winds through the trees and you can feel the energy, the positive energy from nature. You can feel it all around you, penetrating your body and relaxing you deeply, and you feel a new energy, a new energy in your body that affects the way you think, the way you feel, the way you behave, and now it really does feel good.

As you walk along this narrow path, sunlight shining through the canopy above, and it seems to dance upon the ground all around you. You know, now, these things relax you, these things get you thinking, they pass through your thoughts. They get you thinking about the changes that you know down deep that it's time to change.

Feel what it's like, on that deep level to have that stirring take place. Now it's time to change the way you think about yourself, people, places, things, and events. Change how you think about them. Change how you act, overreact, under react.

What is your perception about things that possibly seem one way, but they are really another way? In this other way, what can you do to make changes, to understand these ways in a way you can make changes in the way you think and the way you feel and the way you behave?

Explore the changes that need to be made in your attitude, changes in your perception of the battles of your life. Now, imagine what it would feel like to let go of old beliefs, old behaviors, old processes as you now journey through this path in this forest of your life, in this forest of change.

And as you walk, for quite some time, feeling good, discovering things about yourself deep inside, changing things in the way you think in your mind, changing the way your attitude is. Just let yourself imagine what it's going to be like when you free yourself of these old ways that have been standing between you and freedom.

You come to the edge of the tree line, and there in front of you, is this beautiful meadow. It's quite big, the sun shining bright, white puffy clouds drifting through a blue sky. And there is this meadow covered with these beautiful red flowers, wildflowers, a carpet of red flowers, the red flowers glistening in the sunlight, it just captivates you as you stand there.

It looks like a painting, a painting of nature, and as you stand there looking at these red flowers, just in awe, you notice, as you look closer, there are patches of yellow flowers sprinkled about, just enough to add a bouquet-look to it. Something nature would do. Nature changes, nature changes.

It changes the way it's painted, it changes the way it's grown, it changes, it restructures. And, as you look closer now, you notice some blue flowers just here and there, blue flowers glistening in the sun like those red and yellow flowers, and you realize there's many dimensions to nature, "many dimensions."

And you decide that you are just going to sit down there and enjoy this beautiful sight. And so, you sit down, you lean back against this log and relax. And you notice as you're looking at this beautiful meadow that there is green grass, another dimension, another beauty of nature and life, and changes that take place in the elements that are involved. And you now begin to focus, you begin to focus on the green grasses and you notice that they are swaying back and forth.

(A short pause before continuing)

There's a gentle, gentle, gentle breeze in the air, you can barely feel it on your face. And the tall grasses are swaying back and forth, as though they are dancing with the red flowers, and the yellow flowers, and the blue flowers. The air is filled with the smell of the different flowers and the smell of the trees and nature itself.

And as you sit there, you notice that you can focus on different things. You can focus on just the beauty in general. Or you can focus on the red flowers, you can cast your attention on the yellow flowers and the blue flowers, or you can notice how the green grasses sway and dance in the breeze.

See, there are many ways at looking at something, there are many aspects to consider when looking at something. And you can change from one aspect to the other, and still enjoy and focus on the surrounding elements; it just depends on your focus.

And, as you sit there, you begin now to notice that right in the middle of that meadow is this big oak tree just sprawling out like it's been growing there for hundreds and hundreds of years, and it captivates you because of its picturesque beauty.

And you begin to focus on a new aspect of this same scene. And there, as you sit there and look at that tree, with the backdrop of the blue sky and the white puffy clouds and the sun shining down on the beautiful flowers around it, your attention, you notice, has shifted. Shifted to another aspect just as important, just as important to the beauty of life itself and that is the tree.

But as you sit there and look at this tree, you begin to look deep into this tree. And you notice there are limbs that are missing, and that's when your eyes drop just a little. And you notice lying underneath the tree and all around it are limbs. Some of them are small, some of them are as big around as your leg and others are only as big around as your finger, but they're lying there on the ground underneath the tree, and you think, how did those limbs get there?

But, you're way back out in the forest; surely no one came along and cut them. But then you notice up in the tree, that it's as though these limbs were torn out of the tree. And then you realize that storms, storms happen in the forest of life. Storms, nature has its own way of pruning people, nature has its own way of pruning life events, nature has its own way of pruning the forest. It sends storms that break off the limbs so that they can feed life itself. And now you begin to wonder, really wonder now.

And you, there this very moment, begin to notice, there on the ground, those limbs that are in all stages of decay. Some of the limbs are quite big, and they still have green leaves on them. Others have decayed all the way down to compost. And someplace between that compost and the ones with the green leaves, you realize that these storms have been going on since the beginning of time, since the beginning of your life, since the beginning of the tree being there.

Storms in nature, storms in life, then you realize something. You begin to realize that in your own life, there are storms. You begin to realize that in your own life nature sends storms in the form of emotional pain and it blows away old thoughts, old beliefs, old attitudes, old dreams, old wants and old desires, it breaks them from the way you think, and from the way you feel, and the way you behave.

But what does nature do with them? Why do you fight nature to hold on to them? Did the tree hold onto the limbs, or did it drop them? And for what purpose, what purpose were these limbs, if nature was to come along and break them off? What purpose were the things, the storm that came into your own life, what purpose was it, if it were just for nature to come and create pain and make changes?

And something magical happens, you sitting there at the edge of this meadow, looking at these beautiful flowers and enjoying them, enjoying the fragrance of the flowers and the trees and the sounds of nature itself, reflecting on your own life. Looking at the tree, noticing the things that have changed in that tree, noticing the broken limbs and the decaying limbs underneath, something magical happens. It's as though you can see down into the earth, like x-ray vision.

You can look right down into the root system and you discover, as you have discovered in your own life, the roots of this tree go deep. And there are as many roots underground as there is growth aboveground. And it just captures you. It's almost like you're in awe, you're exploring the roots of your own identity, while you sit there exploring the roots of that tree.

And as you identify with that tree, you too, have had storms in your life. You too have experienced fallen limbs. And then you realize something as you're sitting there. You notice that the compost from the decayed limbs that have fallen from that tree, the limbs that have fallen from that tree and decayed to compost, the nutrients are actually going down into the ground and the root hairs are picking up the nutrients.

The root hairs are picking up the nutrients and sending them into the roots and into the main trunk and up through the tree, and actually, you notice something else now. That everyplace where a limb had been ripped out of the tree, new growth has come.

And then you realize something. That nature, nature sends forth storms, breaks limbs from trees, drops them on the ground, and decays them so that the tree can grow, so that the tree can grow into a new shape, into a new beauty, into a new form. And it's been doing it since this tree was young. And as it gets older, it continues to feed off of what happened and what it has learned from so long ago, from so long ago.

And you sitting there, looking at your own life, begin to realize perhaps you need to grow from these old behaviors, these old experiences, the past hurt that maybe you didn't understand until this very moment, it's now time for you to grow. Now make a shift, look at what's going on in your own life.

What is it you need to learn from these old behavior patterns which no longer work for you? How will it make you a better person? How will it shape you? How can you use this new information in your future to make your life better? Now, it's time for you to take the next step. The tree took the next step. It didn't fight nature, it didn't fight the storm, and it weathered the storm. It gave up that which it needed to give up, in order to grow and stay beautiful, and picturesque.

And as you look at your own life, as you begin to look at the things which have happened in your own life that's brought you sadness and sorrow, even discontentment, those are the limbs that have been ripped from the way you think. Now, how can you turn them to compost and grow from them? What is it that happened in your own life, that it's now time to use, to make new growth? What is this new growth, this new shape, and this new form?

As you let go of holding on, like that tree let go of the limbs that nature had sent the storm to break so that they could feed that very tree, nature has sent storms in your life. Now it's time to accept the nutrients from that growth, from that pruning, from that change. It's now time to change, it's now time to understand, and it's now time to put new growth in the way you think, in the way you feel, in the way you behave, in the way you plan, in the way you act toward other people and toward yourself.

It's now time to grow, to grow into the future, reshape yourself with a new understanding, with wisdom, with a new attitude, from that wisdom. You, sitting there, on the edge of change, reflect deep into yourself. The past, your childhood, things happened in your childhood. Yes, those were limbs that dropped to the ground of your knowledge. What is it you can learn from them, those experiences? They've lain there long enough now. Look back and grow from them.

Look at your young adulthood, attitudes, and behaviors that you had, things you've done, it's now time to learn from them. Let them decay, let them feed you the wisdom and the knowledge they hold, for nature sent the storm of change for you to grow. Look at your own life; look at it in the present. What limbs do you need to let decay so that you can capture the essence of your wisdom?

The tree did not fight the storm, the tree did not grieve and hold onto or try to possess the limb that nature came to prune. You, too, give up, let it decay. Let the knowledge and the wisdom help you to grow into who you're becoming. Look at your future, how will life be better by learning, by learning and shifting, and changing and growing from the things that happened in your childhood, in your young adulthood? And what is present now, what will be the past and the future? How will it make you a better person?

Is it now time for you to look at your life and let these storms form new growth? Is it now time for you to take a look at who you are and who you've been and make these changes? And look at the things you must do with a new zest, look at the things you must do with a new attitude, look at the things you must do with a new desire to make the changes that you now know it's time to make.

Let yourself become aware of the changes that are taking place. Let yourself become aware of so many things that you are aware that you are unaware of. Let yourself become aware of new wants, new needs, and new desires. Let yourself become aware of whatever it is that you held onto that's kept you held back. Let yourself become aware on a conscious level, on a subconscious level, on a deep spiritual level, that it's now time for your mind, body and spirit to work together and bring peace, harmony and tranquility into your everyday life.

It's now time for your intellect, your education, and your emotions to work in harmony with your mind, body and spirit. It's now time to make changes. Feel what it's like to have this stirring. Feel what it's like to have movement, feel what it's like to accept these new changes, these new ideas into your life. Feel it, feel it, feel it.

I'm going to begin to count from 1 to 5. When I say 5 and only when I say 5 and snap my fingers, will you open your eyes feeling good in every way.

1 - Let that part of you that's in charge of that part of you understand that it's time now to make a change, a deep, spiritual change toward a new way of life.

2 - You understand that deep within you there lies a guide that guides you spiritually into the changes, the changes that you must make to bring happiness, peace and harmony into your life.

3 - Know that you know deep inside of you what you need to do, to do what needs to be done and therefore, you begin to make those changes, that shift, and take on that new feeling, that new responsibility, the new you, it's time, it's time.

4 - Each and every time you hear the sounds of my voice, you'll go 10 times deeper, 10 times faster into a deep state of hypnotic relaxation where you discover new aspects, new worlds, new ways of being, you discover them deep within you. They've been with you all along, and now you can use your intellect, your emotions and your thoughts to explore these new realms.

1 - As you begin to come up now, let the changes take place, the new thoughts, the new knowledge, let them grow and manifest themselves in you in the form of happiness, in the form of a new understanding, in the form of a new way of living.

2 - Coming up now, your eyes becoming moist, your breathing picking up and the sounds of my voice calling you up.

3 - Coming up, breathing picking up, knowing that you know, feeling those feelings, relax deep within you, feelings of contentment, feelings of change, feels good to feel good about feeling good about yourself.

4 - Coming up, feeling good in every way; breathing picking up; over the next week you'll feel better than you have felt in days, weeks, months, perhaps even years, because you have decided to make changes and make them permanently. And

5 - Just open your eyes feeling good in every way. (snap fingers)

Trans-Actual Analysis

Trans-Actual Analysis - Parent, Adult, Child

When helping individuals discover, identify and change destructive behaviors, another one of my first responder tools is Trans-Actual Analysis. In this exercise we begin with the theory that within all of us we have a parent, adult, and a child.

I begin with identifying the main role of each part. I then ask, "Who is running your life in areas which are causing you problems?" When they answer, "The Adult, of course." I then ask; "Is this behavior one of an adult or a child?" After we go through a few of their issues they begin to see who is really in charge of their feelings and actions.

This is an excellent tool when beginning to work with anger. I also use it when working with substance abuse. I will do some board talk with the client and demonstrate how the adult is pretty much non-existent in certain behaviors and areas of their life.

Over the years I have been told by clients they have no control over their anger. People or things just get to them and it just takes over their actions. I will respond that it's much like a child throwing a temper tantrum when they don't get their way. Question: Is this the way you want to be viewed by others?

It becomes a little tough when the client comes to the realization that he has been behaving like an eight year old. I've had many of them tell me that they are actually embarrassing of themselves. This realization helps motivate the individual to learn how to make the much needed change.

The Parent

The Parent's main role is to keep us in line and this is usually done by criticizing. Much of this internal dialogue is rooted in childhood. These internal beliefs of what we

Trans-Actual Analysis

Role of Each Aspect of Inner-Self

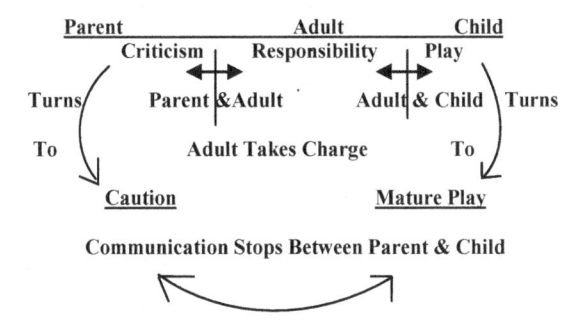

Parent	Adult	Child
Criticism	Responsibility	Play
Turns	Parent & Adult	Adult & Child	Turns
To	Adult Takes Charge	To
Caution		Mature Play

Communication Stops Between Parent & Child

The **Trans-Actual Analysis** illustration will help the Life Coach explain the process of identifying and categorizing certain behaviors expressed by an individual.

should do often clash with what we may want. This programming may have been meant as a positive to protect us from harm or to teach us lessons.

These programmed guilt-producing beliefs include phrases such as do this, do that, don't do that, grow up and act your age, you should know better than that, a grown adult with children staying out that late or spending that much money on yourself when the kids could use clothes or shoes or whatever, for a few examples.

These beliefs may not have been told to us directly; they may, in fact, have been inferred. As our parents or other authority figures make comments about others in our presence, we can and do take these comments to heart. It can be very difficult for us to determine how we came to believe a particular belief because it was inferred.

Many years ago, I was going to do "something," but I don't remember exactly what it was. A girlfriend I had at the time said to me, "You can't do that!" and I asked, "Why not?" She replied "I don't know, you just don't do things like that." What I found surprising was, she had no idea "why not" and no inclinations to even question her belief of, "You just don't do things like that."

Even though the parent within is the one doing the criticizing of our behavior, overall, we are left with feelings of guilt. It seems as though we take over from where the authority figures in our childhood left off. After the "child within" rebels and does what he wants, takes a break and lets off a little steam, the "internal parent" reenters the scene and criticizes self for being irresponsible.

This, of course, creates deep feelings of guilt even though at the time it may not be recognized as such. This battle cycles time and time again without the individual being aware of what is taking place. It is much like the teenager rebelling against the parents, only here it is all taking place internally.

The subconscious programming during childhood can cause this internal battle which may be very difficult to identify and stop without an effective tool. Many of these criticisms may have never actually been said directly to us; they just may have been inferred. That is why they are so difficult to discover and reframe.

When attempting to discover and correct something that was inferred, it can be much like trying to hit a moving target. The target seems to be there, but as you approach or think you are getting close, then it's not there but it feels like it's still there. Behaviors stemming from direct assaults may not be recognized and connected to this internal conflict. Using the Trans-Actual Analysis tool will certainly help reveal many of these issues so they may be reframed.

The Adult

The Adult's role is one of being responsible. However, the internal conflict between the child and the parent overshadows the adult. The adult is left out of the equation for the most part, leaving the parent to criticize and the child to run amok and bring havoc into the individual's life.

Taking responsibility for one's actions without making excuses can be very difficult. This is especially true when the child within has not matured and the criticizing parent hasn't been tempered down and been put in its' place. The adult's part in this play between the parent and the child is to buffer the criticism from the parent and also temper the rebellion from the child.

An example of this behavior would be you (the child) go out one night "to play" and then have a little too much to drink. At the end of the evening you get behind the wheel of your car while intoxicated and drive home. Of course, an adult would not demonstrate such behavior. Clearly, the immature child is running the show (your life).

Although you may have made it home without an encounter with law enforcement or better yet an accident, the adult within was clearly not in charge. The excuse that others do it all of the time just reinforces how the child is in charge.

The inner child has not matured enough to say I'm in no condition to drive. Here, you have your immature child running your life. As you begin looking inside yourself you may find this is also true in many other aspects of your life.

The next day when you return to your "good" senses you may in fact experience feelings of guilt because that inner parent begins making those subconscious remarks to the inner child. What if you had been stopped, or wrecked the car, or hurt someone; you should know better than that.

And you do know better, but the inner child was running the show. This would be especially true if you would have injured someone or been stopped by law enforcement or damaged your car.

To the Life Coach, when using the Trans-Actual Analysis tool, here are a few questions you may want to explore with your client: Who or what is running your life? Why? Are these the actions of an adult? Why? Where is the adult? Why? What is keeping the adult from being responsible and in charge all of the time? Why? It is the adult's responsibility to mature the inner child.

The Child

The role of the Child is to play. Children play differently as they pass through several stages on their way to adulthood. As we age, our inner child still needs to play to let off the pressures of everyday life. This playing alters its characteristics and include a wide variety of involvements, work, sex, hobbies, and parties, just to mention a few.

As we pass through puberty many irresponsible behaviors and beliefs sneak through into adulthood. These beliefs and behaviors can wreak havoc in our private and public affairs. Because proper corrections were not made early on, we have no other experiences to compare them to so they can feel quite normal.

Without being recognized by the individual, these immature behaviors can cost relationships, jobs and, for many, a host of legal problems. In reality what is happening, when triggered, our childhood emotions and programming take control of our actions and behaviors in many areas of our lives.

When childhood emotions are in charge, it is easy to develop the attitude that because I'm an "adult" nobody can tell me what to do. We either are not aware or don't care that we live in a society of rules. For many of us when we break those rules and get caught we feel guilty.

This guilt feeling is a form of the parent within scolding the child within. This internal battle can continue throughout an individual's life or until he seeks help in making corrections. These corrections include maturing the inner child, thus, putting the adult in charge.

The more the adult is in control the better the decisions. Keep in mind, the child is not going to give up control easily. As the adult takes charge, the inner parent's criticism turns to caution by the adult making more mature and balanced decisions as well as taking actions that create a more harmonious life.

The adult no longer gives in to childish feelings and urges that may create problems. This taking control by the adult begins the maturing of the inner child. The parent no longer needs to create feelings of guilt because the adult behaves responsibly.

The adult now takes the criticism of the parent as caution without the feelings of guilt. The adult gives attention to the inner child's need and sees that he is not deprived of fun and play. This helps create balance in the individual's life.

This process or journey into self must be a conscious decision and it requires a conscious effort until the old programs are changed. It is also an awareness of the programming that what they have come to believe is not working to their advantage and must be changed.

With a clear understanding of the Trans-Actual Analysis Tool, the Life Coach can lead the client through a wide array of issues awakening him to a more profound view of himself and others. Used in conjunction with other tools in this manual, the process will help the client with self-esteem and self-confidence building.

Sources of Stress

Many experiences, situations, and issues may contribute to stress. To better understand and deal with them, I have found it helpful if they are categorized. There are a variety of stressors which we have little or no control over. However, the way we approach each can make a difference in the way we are affected.

Those seemingly out of control stressors can wreak havoc in our lives to the point of causing fears, phobias, panic attacks, and a long list of other illnesses. Even the people we love and things we like to do cause us stress. Acquiring and using the proper tools can go a long way when neutralizing stress.

Each individual will have their own version of what is stressing them out. As I listen to my clients, I will begin organizing their stressors into categories on the whiteboard.

I will also ask questions and make suggestions about how they are being affected by stress. I explain to them that we will use four main categories.

The first category we will discuss is Progressive Accumulating Stress. This is everyday stress which continues to mount and wear us down. It seems to get worse before we have time to figure out how to resolve it. In many cases it may seem like there is no resolve; we're just stuck in a miserable rut.

The next category is those Anticipated Events which we may look forward to but are stressful just the same. Coupled with the Progressive Stressors the pressures mount until we feel things are more than we can handle. Categorizing in this manner can help the individual get a better understanding of the stressors in his life and help him to do some prioritizing.

Our next category is Unexpected Events which may cripple us emotionally and/or financially. These are the ones which we dread and may seem to come out of nowhere. In this category we have absolutely no control over what happens.

Finally, we come to the Self-Imposed Stressors which we do have control over, or at least we can gain control over. These are the ones which are Self-Imposed. These Self-Imposed stressors can alter how we perceive the other events and situations which we may encounter.

Progressive Accumulating Stress

Progressive Accumulating Stress is rooted in our daily lives. Work can be very stressful especially when you work at a job for which you are not best suited. It may appear the pressures never seem to let up no matter how hard you work.

An example of this would be when a predominately right-brained person is attempting to do a left-brain job or vice versa. Keep in mind the right brained individual is conceptual, creative and timeless. The left-brained individual is logical, sequential, and orderly in thought.

When you are a left-brain person in a situation where you have to be creative and your creativity doesn't flow easily or freely, because the stress is progressive, it's only a matter of time until you begin to experience problems either in your health or relationships or both.

The same holds true when you are a right-brained person and very creative and conceptual in thought but force yourself to be logical and sequential in thought. You will struggle to perform daily, and this will be a major source of progressive stress in your life.

You may be working at a job or company or for a boss that you simply do not like. It is a possibility that you have outgrown your job or career and have simply become bored. This can be very stressful, especially if you do not have the education or training or desire to make a career change.

Even if you do have the skills you need to change careers, it still can be stressful to give up seniority and start at a lesser pay for a new company with new co-workers, and all the other stress that comes with changing jobs.

I've learned from years of doing hypnotherapy, and in life as well, that friction between parents and children can go way back into childhood. These conflicts may carry into adulthood and even into senior years. These unresolved issues require a massive amount of our energy to keep them repressed.

People may be unaware of this energy drain because the inner conflict has been with them for so long it feels normal and, therefore, goes unnoticed. However, these unresolved issues are expressed in other areas of life, such as a lack of tolerance for others, impatience, anger issues, or other behavioral problems.

On a daily basis, while raising children, the stress is progressive and accumulating. Because children are constantly changing, the parents must change as well. Should there be a problem child or a special needs child in the family, the stress is magnified. Broken homes can cause issues between the children and their parents and in turn create a progressive stress that the child or parent does not know how to handle.

Anticipated Events

Anticipated Events also can be very stressful. For example, you may spend several years going to college which can be stressful in and of itself; however, anticipating graduating can actually be even worse as the reality draws near because then you have to find a job and perform hoping you retained what you need to prosper.

Anticipated events in your life can range from getting married to having children and even retirement. Upon retiring, learning to live on a fixed income or feelings of no longer being useful or needed can cause undue emotional stress. These events or similar ones will happen, and there is nothing we can do about it but learn to handle them in a positive manner.

Unexpected Events

Unexpected Events can be devastating stressors to anyone, but for most of us they will still likely happen. Being a victim of a crime, an unexpected loss of a job, being diagnosed with a serious illness, death of a loved one; all can leave us with feelings of hopelessness. Seldom do any of us possess the tools it takes to adequately deal with such experiences.

These thoughts can play over and over in our minds and can have a negative effect on us for years. Also, there are many negative behaviors which may be brought on from the repressed feelings and emotional pain attached to these experiences.

Repressed and suppressed feelings tear at the very fabric of who we are as human beings. As a Life Coach you may find it very beneficial to explore this area in your client's life as the two of you journey beyond the symptoms and behavioral patterns he may be experiencing. Reframing these events can be very favorable.

Personal Trait Stress

Here is where the action and changes take place. To make changes in one's belief system, their self-esteem, and self-image requires an individual to come to certain realizations. What they were taught in their childhood and how they understood what they had learned, may not be working for them as an adult. It may actually be the source of their problems and negative behaviors.

Low self-esteem can be caused by a series of direct assaults, as well as ones that were inferred. Many of these verbal and non-verbal accusations can reinforce low self-esteem and a poor self-image. Initially this can be brought about by the way we were treated and by what was taught to us when we were very young.

The inferred assaults may be learned by the way parents and family talk about the behaviors and actions of others. This infers to us, that if later in life we happen to encounter something of that nature, no matter how we may handle the issue, it will be wrong. This, of course, has a negative effect on our self-esteem and self-image.

Later in life as the individual attempts to use those "inferred beliefs," of which he is consciously unaware, he subconsciously begins to identify with those inferred judgment comments made by others. Rather than questioning what he was taught and what he has come to believe as fact, he assumes down deep he is the person with the problem.

These misconceptions and misinformation within his belief system, in many cases, can lead him to create self-imposed perfectionism, feelings of insecurity, lack of confidence, low self-esteem, a negative or poor self-image, jealousy, guilt, and feelings of inadequacy, just to mention a few.

When we are young our subconscious takes everything as truth. It is a "yes" mind, especially when we are young and have no experiences to compare what we are being taught. We just simply believe what we are told by "those who know."

Keep in mind, many of the "facts and beliefs" that we are taught as young children are an accumulation of other people's beliefs, wants, and desires. They are still taught to us even though these "facts and beliefs" do not work for the ones doing the teaching. Many of these teachings are idealistic and have little to do with reality.

The people who are doing the teaching include parents, clergy, teachers, and authority figures. Society in general also plays a major role. Their intentions may be good and honorable but since they convey so many mixed messages, they cause problems in an individual's life.

Some of these issues are mishandled as they begin to develop in childhood and adolescence. Many other problems are revealed when the individual becomes an adult and begins having problems in his personal and/or professional life.

Armed with all of these mixed messages, untruths, and idealistic beliefs we are sent out into the world on our own to prove, or in some cases disprove, our beliefs. When these beliefs fail us, we are left with personal trait stress and have nowhere to go but inside and question our own self-worth.

These beliefs can go unchallenged for years. I have found it amazing that even though a person's beliefs have not worked for many years, they still are either unwilling or are afraid to challenge and change them. They seem to believe that is the way they are and nothing can be done to change what they have come to believe as truth.

I ask, "Even though you can't seem to keep a job or a long-term relationship and have been told on several occasions that it's because of your attitude, you remain afraid of change. What in the world do you have to lose? It sounds to me like you have everything to gain."

In many cases, the response has been, "What if I find out that I'm a bad person or no good or worthless or something bad that can't be changed? How can I deal with myself?" I always quickly respond without hesitation, "It does not work that way." I then go on and explain to them that the very fact you are here on this earth as a living being means you are a good person or you would not be here.

"Your spirit is pure. You are a spiritual being having a physical experience. Part of your journey is to find your true self, not what you are left with after years of being programmed with misinformation. This internal journey involves using all of your life's experiences to accomplish that realization of self."

I then go on to explain about the programming that takes place when we are young. Part of our journey on this earth is to right all of our wrong beliefs, or at least as many as we can. This is what creates wisdom. This is one of the reasons I refer to this process as a spiritual journey.

Self-Imposed Perfectionism
Self-Imposed Perfectionism is one of the key culprits in this category. I can't tell you how many times I've heard someone say, "I'm a perfectionist" or "He or she is a perfectionist." There is a huge difference between excellence and perfection. Since everything can be improved upon, nothing is perfect. When building the

space shuttle, as high-tech as "it" is, the people building it worked within certain tolerances.

This need for perfection, rather than excellence, leads to low self-esteem and little to no creativity. Since "nothing is perfect," the perfectionist is in a constant state of conflict and stress. This need for approval actually gives away the person's power without them being aware of what is happening.

Mistakes are viewed as failures rather than a learning experience. These individuals become critics rather than creators. Having pride in what you are engaged in and doing your best is one thing, but taking simple tasks to extreme is something else.

The Perfectionist
The perfectionist may want to evaluate the purpose and value of the project and the impact it has on what is really important to him or her. He or she may find that they are losing friends and loved ones because of their lack of "tolerance." It is important to know when excellence, and not perfection, is the order of the day and to know that good enough is "good enough."

The perfectionist may want to journey back into his life to find how and why and who was involved with him "becoming this way." Then determine just how "perfect" those people who influenced him were. He may be pleasantly surprised to find those people had their own issues which they have successfully disguised. Here is something to think about: What if humans are perfect being imperfect?

Insecurity

Insecurity is another issue in this category. Self-doubt and the lack of confidence go hand-in-hand. Being insecure about how you look, your weight, height, the color of your hair, or complexion may cause a variety of overcompensating behaviors which bring about other problems in a person's life.

The key here is, for the Life Coach to find the areas in an individual's life where they are insecure and make some changes by reframing the issues involved. Of course, this may require some effort. In most cases there is no quick fix. There is no pill. It may require going back to school, no matter what the age. It may require extra studying or even learning how to study.

It may require sacrifice of family or recreational time. It may require going to the gym and working with a personal trainer. It may require an extensive amount of reading or research on a certain subject. Whatever it is that a person is insecure about can be changed. My experience is that it usually takes a lot of effort.

One of my favorite sayings that I have used most of my adult life is, "First, you have to want to, not like to, not wish to, but really want to." You must "Want To" bad enough that you would do whatever it takes to make these changes in your life and accomplish your desired outcome.

Many times we have to create that want. We have to find what is holding us back, learn from it, and free up that energy to take on more complex and difficult issues. I've always believed if we get off the sofa and do our part, the universe will do its part and provide a way. This is much like *"when the student is ready, the teacher will appear."*

Insecurity will have a direct negative effect on how we view and handle any progressive, customary, and unexpected life events. Personal Trait Stress is the starting point in resolving problems in most areas of life. It is not always what has happened to us but how we handle what has happened.

One of the first steps in resolving insecurity is trust. This means trusting yourself enough to metaphorically go inside yourself and take a look around. The next part is being honest with yourself about what you see. Here you make no excuses; just observe and be completely honest. For balance, it is important to look at both your positive and negative aspects.

It is then important to respond by tracing the insecurity back to its beginning and beyond. When the root cause is discovered, you can take action by doing what it takes to rid yourself of the insecurity. This may mean you have to let go of anger, feelings of abandonment, and/or betrayal. This can be accomplished by reframing each component of the issue.

It also may require forgiveness of someone that you feel you have the right to be angry with but who doesn't deserve your forgiveness. Keep in mind, that you also have the right not to be angry. Since anger is an active emotion, it will eat its way out of you, so you owe it to yourself to let it go.

This process of ridding oneself of insecurity works well with other aspects of personal trait stress. Insecurity is best friends with other personal trait stressors such as Poor Self-Image, Jealousy, Lack of Confidence, Feelings of Inadequacy, and Guilt.

The Life Coach must help the client pick one of the aspects of his insecurity and trace it back to its origin. He then guides the client through the process of finding when and why it began and then begins the reframing process. This will take a little more work and some soul-searching, but it's well worth the journey.
(Refer to Reframing)

Here the client learns to accept the uniqueness of the characteristics he brought with him to this earth. This is learning to love himself for whom he is and the qualities he possesses. The next part is for him to be willing to change the things which he controls. This, too, will require a little more work.

Positive Attainment

Denial – Anger – Action

Attainment is a process of going in a positive direction. It is a way of creating a positive and healthy outcome in any given situation. At times, it may be difficult to adjust to the changes which are taking place. It is also a process of taking charge of any given situation even though it may be difficult and painful.

The Denial, Anger, Action process is a tool I use to help the client achieve emotional movement usually from a state of denial or anger into a state of action. An individual can experience all three at the same time. They may simply be in a state of denial about the severity of a situation where they have found themselves. They may be lying to themselves and making excuses for the situation they are in, or the person to whom they are angry towards, which is also "a form of denial."

Rather than owning the problem and taking action to resolve the issue, they blame others or circumstances and maintain a position of denial or anger. The action to which they may deem as the only way out of the mess they are in may be too difficult or simply unacceptable.

It may be an action they are unwilling to take at the present time. Whichever the case they remain in their particular position until something happens that forces them to take action. They still remain in a defensive position instead of taking an offensive action.

Rather than address an issue at its onset, we tend to put it off and hope it goes away or gets better on its own. As the issue begins to escalate, we have a tendency to put off addressing it until the "right" time. Many times, we may fear that addressing it might actually cause it to get worse. Then as it worsens, we begin to make excuses, even to the point of denying that it is, in fact, a problem.

To us, these excuses seem to be legitimate, because addressing the problem may cause us to lose a relationship, lose our job, or even lose a way of life that we have worked so hard to achieve. Fearing the action may result in negative consequences, we go into denial. This seems to work for a while.

However, when a problem is not addressed, seldom does it get better; it only continues to get worse. Not dealing with the problem may even create an undercurrent. This can cause the issue to come out in life as problems or behaviors which may not seem related to why we are in denial.

It's not long until we move from denial into anger or a state of fear, depending on the situation. Becoming angry, we may let off a little steam by "blowing our stack." We then go back to our excuses, using phrases like "it doesn't matter anyway; perhaps I'm being a little over sensitive."

These excuses let us slip back into denial. However, we can't go completely back into denial because on some level we have emotionally accepted there is, in fact, a problem. Because it may involve others or another person, we just are not sure of the best way to resolve the issue.

At this particular time in the process it may not seem worth losing whatever it is that we have accomplished. The problem remains and slowly worsens. Something happens and we shift again from denial and deeper into anger. Looming in the shadows of our mind is the never-ending presence of having to take an action that we deem unacceptable.

The feelings and emotions attached to this anger begin to take control of the situation and, we may attempt to negotiate with the other party. We may even agree on some common ground. However, unless behaviors and actions that lead up to these deep-seated issues are resolved, the problem will remain.

These feelings and emotions may be suppressed and repressed for years, causing a variety of problems in our life. My experience is that, for many individuals, they do not believe experiences in the past have anything to do with the emotional or physical problems of the present.

I have also heard them say that they have put those issues in the past, or that they have forgotten about those things and they no longer matter. The problem with this type of reasoning is their inner-child still feels the pain from those past issues. They have become so used to the pain they simply ignore it on a conscious level.

The problem will continue to get worse even though they may try to see the other person's point of view and use that as a course to head back into denial thinking, "It Won't Work." It's not long until some incident "pulls the trigger" and back deep into heated anger they go. Here they begin to face the reality that something has to be done differently. However, the action that they feel must be taken, may still be unacceptable.

It has been my experience that for many people they seem to become frozen in this angry state of mind. Not having the resources, the self-esteem, confidence, or the knowledge to take the action that they believe would correct the problem, "they remain stuck." They may continue to direct their anger at a particular person or event.

However, with some self reflection, they soon realize on a deep inner level that they are angry at themselves for not recognizing what has been taking place. Also, they may be angry for letting themselves get into the situation in the first place.

Positive Attainment

Denial - Anger - Action

Denial	Anger	Action
		Unacceptable Solution
		↓
		Accepted or
		↓
		New Solution

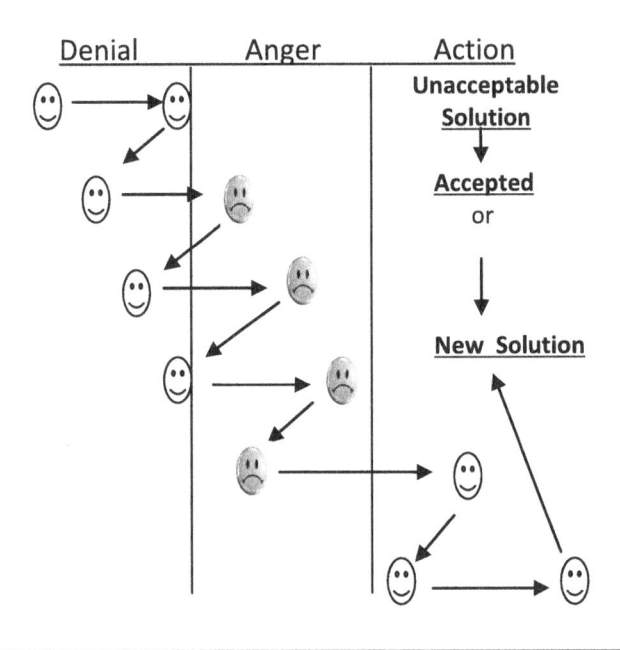

The illustration shows the thought process from **Denial** to **Action**. There are individuals that remain stuck in a state of **Anger** while others may attempt to remain in **Denial** for various reasons.

Denial

Many people use denial as a coping tool. However, when denial is used as a way of coping, the problem will always find a way to surface. In my own family, for example, when my uncle passed away, his daughter was unable to deal with the pain of the loss of her dad. She could not bear to come to the funeral. One day we were talking and she explained to me that she just pretends that he is away on business because she couldn't deal with the fact that he was not here with us anymore.

While I was in Shenyang, China doing management training for some companies, my interpreter mentioned her husband was working in Beijing. When we were supposed to leave for Beijing the next day, I asked if she was going to spend time with her husband while we were there and, if so, who would I use as an interpreter since I didn't speak Chinese. Very solemnly she explained her husband had died ten years ago and that she just pretends he's in Beijing working.

Recently a woman came to me and wanted to know if hypnosis could help her stop grinding her teeth. She stated she had been grinding her teeth for quite some time, day and night, and it was driving her crazy and damaging her teeth. I asked her, "How's your home life?" She explained to me that she and her husband are happily married, have always gotten along well together, and both are retired.

She told me that her home life was fine and that the teeth grinding had nothing to do with her home life. I explained that perhaps her subconscious had created this teeth grinding as a distraction so she wouldn't have to deal with something that she does not know how to cope with in her life.

I further explained that we would have to dig a little deeper and find out what "that something is." Together we would then help her to find a way to face the situation. I explained to her the teeth grinding is only a symptom of a deeper issue. There were other signals in her body language and facial expressions that revealed a deeper problem.

As we continued to talk she informed me that her husband has Alzheimer's but that it wasn't that bad and they were planning a trip abroad. She began to reveal that her husband had gotten lost in the neighborhood a couple of times and the police had brought him home.

I mentioned that if he was going to continue to go for walks alone, that perhaps she might get some sort of GPS locating device in case he got lost again, that it would certainly take a lot of worry away from her. Very soberly she explained it wasn't that bad, that it had only happened a couple of times.

As we continued to talk, she mentioned that one day he was searching for something in the house and looking through cupboards. When she asked him what he was looking for, he told her that he was trying to find the garbage disposal.

She told me she just couldn't believe that he did not know where the garbage disposal was located. A few weeks later when she came to her appointment, I asked how things were going and she broke down crying and said "Not well." I asked, "What is the problem?" She said they had gone to dinner with their daughter and both of them had noticed he was confused on how to use the silverware.

She said "I've been in denial all this time, it's much worse than I wanted to believe, I don't know what to do. I'm afraid I'm going to lose my house, I'm afraid I'm not going to have enough money to live on, I'm afraid I won't have the means to take care of him or have him taken care of, I don't know what to do."

For quite some time, she had been living in her world of denial, but reality was quickly setting in on a conscious level. On a deep, subconscious level she knew what was taking place and how she would be affected. Not being equipped to handle what was happening in her life on a conscious level, her subconscious created a distraction.

That distraction was the grinding of her teeth. I explained to her, it's important to accept what is taking place in her life and take some type of assertive action, rather than being angry and fearful, for it is in action and only in action, where you will find relief.

To help move her into action, we discussed several issues concerning her finances, her legal rights, and the actions that needed to be taken. A few of those actions included doing an inventory of her assets, contacting an attorney, dealing with the Veteran's Administration, etc.

I was giving her homework so she could be taking action and educating herself while finding possible solutions. I explained to her that no matter what, the outcome will not be good, but at least we can answer many of the unknowns which will bring her some relief, and then time and therapy will do the rest.

During her sessions, we did hypnosis to help relieve the stress. While she was in hypnosis I gave her ego-strengthening suggestions, as well as direct post-hypnotic suggestions, to stop the teeth grinding. I made suggestions for her to replace her negative thoughts with thoughts and memories of good times.

I included happy times she had revealed during our pre-talk. Also, I gave her suggestions to help her conscious mind accept what was taking place in her life. Those suggestions included that as she took action in preparing for what is coming, she would no longer need distractions from the truth. After a few months the teeth grinding began to subside.

It is important the Life Coach listen for that unique state of denial and stay ready to address it as gently as possible. This is especially necessary in a case that is severe enough for the client to create physical distractions. It is very important to separate a symptom from the real problem.

In the case mentioned above, the client came to me because of teeth grinding, but in reality that was just a symptom of an underlying problem. I believe if I had worked with just the teeth grinding and not found the underlying issue, we would have had little to no success.

Anger

Anger is like acid: sooner or later it will eat its way through its container. Since Anger is an active state of emotion it will eat its way out of you. It will destroy your health in some way and/or destroy your relationships. It can cause weight gain or weight loss, depending on the individual. It can be associated with many chronic conditions that you may never suspect have anything to do with anger.

For many individuals Anger brings with it a sense of entitlement. Over the years I have had many people tell me they have a right to be angry and a right to hold on to it. They seem to wear it like a badge of honor while it continues to eat away at them.

A few years ago, the manager of a company that I was consulting for, sent one of their supervisors to me for anger management. We began to get deeper into his life and his perceptions of why he would get so angry. I asked what he thought it would take to eliminate this out-of-control emotion. After a considerable amount of dialogue he finally said, "I wouldn't know who I am without my anger."

I have found for most adults who have anger issues the anger is within them and is usually based as far back as their childhood. Other people or certain situations simply push their buttons and they "blow up." The need of the want of control or want of approval can be a basis for their anger.
(Refer to Control/Approval, Behavior Patterns and Control Dramas)

When addressing Anger issues, the Life Coach will attempt to trace the behavior back to a time before the client had Anger issues. Perhaps they have no recollection of a time when they weren't angry. (Make note of situations and circumstances they encountered as they grew up.)

Parents divorcing, being passed around to family members, feelings of being neglected; all of these and many more, can play a role in their deep-seated Anger issues. There will need to be some serious and thorough Reframing in the case of deep-seated anger. The Life Coach will need to be innovative and use every tool at hand to neutralize deep-seated anger.

Action

Here is where the work begins. Finding the resolve within oneself to change a belief or situation, perhaps give up a good paying job, or possibly leaving a relationship which they have built so many hopes and dreams on, can be very difficult, to say the least.

To find other alternatives requires an individual to look inside themselves, take inventory, and address the beliefs that are holding them back from achieving their dreams in life. Although it may sound difficult, they may only need to change the way they perceive what is causing them to be angry in the first place.

Tweaking one's core beliefs can be scary for most people. This may require them to change careers or obtain a college degree or something else that takes time, money, and a considerable amount of effort. Whatever the case, the pressure will continue to build until some sort of action is taken.

Rather than embark upon a journey into self in search of the issues and the solutions, many individuals turn to prescription or illegal drugs to cope. However, they know on some level, that the drugs are a band-aid and not the solution to their emotional distress.

When confronted with taking responsibility for the inner conflict, their critical faculty has a tendency to immediately throw out anything that is in direct opposition to their belief system. Although the Critical Faculty is set up as a safeguard it can also keep us stuck within a belief which is not working in our best interests.
(Refer to Critical Faculty located in Mind Levels)

When assisting the client in finding a solution to his issues, the Life Coach's position is to help the client explore many alternatives. The client must discover how and why those alternatives may, and may not, resolve the problem. When action is taken, it can affect others in a positive or negative way. The client must take into consideration how they will handle the fallout.

Not long ago I had a client come to me with a number of issues, one of which was she had broken up with her fiancé of several years because she had become bored with him. She said it seemed like all they did was work and they didn't go out and have fun anymore and she missed him. She was surprised when she was no longer considered a member of his family.

She told me that she was lonely and had no friends because she had made his friends her friends and now no one calls. She said she felt uncomfortable being around them, especially when he was there with his new girlfriend. She had made the comment that she didn't see why she and her ex could not be friends and do things together and still visit "their friends." Here is a good example of someone taking action without considering the fallout.

Control Dramas

The Quest for Power
Intimidator – Interrogator – Aloof – Poor Me

When I use this tool with individuals, couples or families, I am simply bringing to their attention the hurtful game they are playing with each other. I also help them to determine which role each of them promotes. Each person has their own particular role which they play out, both in their personal and professional relationships.

To get the clients' attention and to get us all on the same page, I begin by asking the questions: "What does an Intimidator/Bully need?" (I pause) I then answer, "A Poor Me/Victim." I then ask: "What does a Poor Me/Victim need in order to be a victim?" I answer, "An Intimidator." Then to lighten things up a little I will then say, "Now here is a perfect match; a match made in heaven or hell, depending on how you look at it."

I also bring to their attention that each role hurts both the person playing the role and the person being acted upon, "the Victim." In the short-term, the individual who is the target and in the line of fire, gets hurt. In the long-term, the perpetrator gets hurt because he unwittingly pushes the people he cares about away because of his actions and behaviors.

I explain the characteristics of each role and how they interact with one another. Together we work to find a way to break the behavior patterns of each individual and stop this game of pain. This involves going back and visiting some of their childhood issues and reframing some of the things that have taken place.

As very young children, we begin to search for ways to get our wants and needs met. This search is a struggle for power. If the behaviors stemming from this struggle are not brought into check during those early developmental years they will cause a variety of problems later in the individual's life.

Depending on the family dynamics or the particular situation of the child-rearing environment, these behaviors create an undercurrent and surface subtly later in life as problems in their relationships, both personal and professional.

On a surface level, the individual may actually get his immediate desires met. However, he may not realize the extent of the long-term personal cost. The behaviors he exemplifies will seem normal and acceptable to him because he has been "that way" most of his life.

A disservice may have been done to him by the adults in his life because many times the adults in charge of teaching and being a role model have the same problem. Or, they may have some other overpowering behaviors which create the behavior he will be stuck with for years to come.

Here, I will explain the four major Control Dramas and how they interact with one another. Although I use the term "him or he," this also applies to the female gender.

Control Dramas
Power Game

Intimidator
Outer Behavior:
Denial of fault, Easily agitated and angered,
Me first attitude, Arrogant.
Inner struggle:
Fear of loss of control, Feels no one cares for him,
Fear of not having enough of anything.

Interrogator
Outer Behavior:
Constantly questioning, Who do you think you are?
Where are you going? Why this, Why that?
Inner Struggle:
You must realize you need me and I need you,
You must prove your love, People leave me and I'm afraid you will.

Aloof
Outer Behavior:
I'm not ready to answer or respond,
I don't know for sure, I'm not sure.
Inner Struggle:
I don't necessarily know what I feel or think,
I'm afraid to be wrong.

Poor Me
Outer Behavior:
You don't have to worry about me, I'll be fine,
It's not my fault, it's just the way I am,
poor me I'll do it.
Inner Struggle:
No one sees all the good I do, I need recognition,
If I change you won't love me.

This illustration lays out the basics of the Control Drama. It gives the Life Coach an insight into certain behaviors and their categories so they may be brought to an individual's awareness with a possibility for change.

Intimidator

The Intimidator's outer behavior is one of denial. Nothing will ever be his fault even when it is obvious. Seldom, if ever, will he listen to any one or take any type of criticism, even though it may be constructive and could actually help him.

He will be quickly and easily angered. He will also have an air of arrogance with a "me first" attitude. He tends to operate in a zone of controlled rage; this is where his anger quickly goes over the top. This particular drama is also very prone to violence in order to back up his behavioral threats.

Keep in mind, these negative behaviors seem perfectly normal to him because they started so early in his childhood. Back then they actually got him what he wanted in his family. If he is now called out on these behaviors, his reply is "This is just the way I am," or some other negative comment.

The Intimidator's inner struggle is somewhat broad and is seated in fear and being a victim. He will have a major fear of being controlled. As you dig deeper into what makes him tick, you will also find a severe fear of not having enough, no matter how much he has or how much he has accomplished.

Another fear he will be dealing with is no one noticing or caring about him. He believes that he has to "do it alone" because no one can ever "do it" right or good enough. He also has a deep feeling that no one ever really took care of him.

All of these inner struggles that he is subconsciously dealing with makes others feel angry toward him. They are afraid to get close to him because they don't know what might set him off next. These responses only fuel the fire and make matters worse.

Because of the way he treats others, they also feel vengeful and are always looking for his weak point. He either does not care or he is completely clueless that he makes others feel negated by his behaviors. He also doesn't seem to realize they will retaliate when given the opportunity.

Most of the Intimidators that I have encountered seem to pride themselves in their ability to intimidate and manipulate others. They are aware of what they are doing, as it gives them a feeling of superiority and power over others, especially in the work place.

Some years back as a consultant, I would go to corporations and teach Team Building. I discovered when an "Intimidator" manager was up against a crucial time line and his job was on the line, he never had the cooperation of his crew.

It was revealed to me privately, on several occasions, that this lack of cooperation was because of the way they had been treated by him. His crew had the attitude that "his day would come" and he would find out what it was like to be treated in this manner.

The matching dramas that are affected by the Intimidator include all four dramas: Intimidator, Interrogator, Aloof and Poor Me. Each one has an internal response to the Intimidator and his behaviors. These responses may or may not necessarily be expressed verbally.

The Poor Me response is to withdraw in fear as to quietly say, "Please don't hurt me, I'm not threatening to you, and

I will not fight back. I am the victim here and will not challenge you."

The Interrogator's internal response, which also may be verbal, "You don't scare me; you're not as powerful as you think you are or act. In fact, it won't be long before I find your weak point." This is the vengeful approach to the Intimidator.

The Aloof response is seldom verbal he just simply will not respond or confront the Intimidator. He takes the stance of silence, leaving the Intimidator to sort out what he may be thinking or what action he may take. This is the negated approach.

Some time back, I received a call from a man who was referred to me by another client. He said his wife had left him and he was coming apart. This call came in on a Friday afternoon, so I told him I could see him Monday morning. He replied that he didn't think he could make it until Monday, so I told him I would see him first thing Saturday morning.

As we began to talk he explained that he could not focus at work, he could not sleep, and he could not stop crying. I asked him why he thought his wife had left and he said she told him she was tired of the way he had been treating her. It didn't take but a few minutes to determine he was the Intimidator.

He said he had been running his home the same as he did his crew on the job. That is, if the people who worked for him didn't like the way he ran the job, they could just pack up their tools and he would find someone else. The same went for his wife and children.

He said for years he would get really angry and yell and tell his wife if she didn't like the way he was she could pack her stuff and go. Eventually, that is exactly what she did. She rented an apartment and moved out. He was in total shock that she actually moved.

He asked her if she would go to therapy and work things out and she agreed. During one of the sessions he bragged about how he could intimidate anyone, even me. I just let him talk without responding to this remark. Later, as I was using an analogy referring back to something he had said, he remarked, "See I am intimidating you right now."

At this point I stopped and looked him square in the eyes and said, "You do not intimidate me. I am not going to go hungry from the little bit of money you spend on these sessions. I am trying to save your family. I am doing my best to help you and hopefully have your wife come back home."

"There are multitudes of therapists in town; you do not have to come to see me. We need to be clear about what we are attempting to accomplish here and stay focused." He looked at me for a few seconds with a shocked look on his face and said, "You're right, sorry." I replied, "Okay, let's get back on task."

From that point on things went much smoother and his wife eventually moved back home. He called a few hours after the session and apologized for his behavior. I told him that it was all right and old negative behaviors are hard to confront and change and that I was in fact on his side.

They stopped coming to see me shortly after she moved back home, even though they had not resolved most of their key issues or the fallout that was bound to happen. Several months later, I received a call from him. He said they were having some problems because his wife was trying to deal with feelings of resentment toward him because of the way he had treated her. Resentment is the fallout which they needed to be prepared for, but they chose to stop their sessions before we reached that stage of resolution.

Interrogator

The Interrogator's outer behavior is one of questioning everything and everybody. A few examples are: Who do you think you are? Where are you going? Why are you going there? When will you be back? Why didn't you do "such and such?" Why don't you do this or that? I told you so.

The Interrogator's inner struggle began in childhood and it's one of no acknowledgement as a child. Their inner struggle is based in fear. They have feelings of people leaving them because they are afraid of being alone. The thought of being alone is terrifying to them.

When in a relationship, they are in constant need of proof of love. They live in fear of their significant other leaving them. They need to be assured that they are needed as they let the other person know they are needed. This internal fear constantly keeps them on guard.

These insecurities expressed by the Interrogator make others feel monitored. This monitoring causes others to avoid the Interrogator. It also causes individuals to be aloof when around, or in a relationship with them.

Because of this constant questioning and monitoring, people feel negated by the Interrogator. They have the feeling their wants, needs, and desires do not matter to the selfish Interrogator. However, he doesn't seem to have a clue about the effect he has on them.

People are also left with the feeling they are always wrong in the eyes of the Interrogator because of all the questioning. No matter what they do, it seems impossible to please those insecure individuals. No matter what the answer, the questions just continue.

The matching dramas most affected by the Interrogator are the Aloof and the Poor Me. To combat the continual monitoring, the Aloof remains silent. The silence sends the message to the Interrogator, "You don't know what I'm thinking." It also leaves the Aloof with feelings that the Interrogator is more powerful than he. This causes the Aloof to have feelings of being negated.

From all of the questioning by the Interrogator, the Poor Me constantly has a feeling of being wrong, and to some degree, worthless. His inner dialogue is *some day you will see my true worth.* Keep in mind, the Poor Me's state of mind is that of a victim.

Aloof

The Aloof individual's outer behavior is one of uncertainty. His inner dialogue includes phrases like *I'm not ready to reveal or speak or give my opinion yet.* In order to be right, which is very important to him, he is constantly in a state of mind that he needs more of something more information, more money, more education, or more time.

His inner struggle is that of fear: *I'm afraid I may become trapped, I'm afraid I'll be unable to perform, I'm not sure I will survive that situation or this experience.* This inner struggle may also include the individual really not knowing exactly what he feels.

The Aloof causes others to feel uncertain about him because of his silence. His quiet demeanor also generates a sense of suspicion of him from others. His quietness causes others to think he is upset and/or something is wrong with him or the situation or them.

The matching drama most affected by the Aloof is the Interrogator. This control drama is unique because of the relationship between the Aloof and the Interrogator. Most of us know the saying that opposites attract, however, in this area there can be some real problems.

During my sessions I'm often asked if the Aloof creates the Interrogator by being so quiet or does the Interrogator create the Aloof because of all of the questioning. Even though one may not necessarily create the other, they certainly add to one another's insecurities.

Couples tend to blame each other for their communication problems. She, (the Interrogator), says she would not ask so many questions if he, (the Aloof), would only talk more. She says, she always feels something is wrong or he's angry or upset about something.

He, on the other hand, says he might talk more if she would only stop asking so many questions. He also says he does talk when he has something "important" to say. Nearly every aloof individual that I have worked with says, "I'm not good at small talk, I'm not angry, or upset I just can't think of anything to say."

Poor Me

The Poor Me individual's outer behavior is one of being a victim. His inner dialogue includes phrases such as *I'm so tired; I can't help it, that's just the way I am; Don't blame me, I'm doing the best I can; Don't worry about me, I'll be fine; Here, I'll take care of that, let me do it.*

The Poor Me's inner struggle is also that of a victim. His internal phrases include thoughts such as *I do so much and yet no one sees me; I don't know how to get energy any other way other than being a victim; If I should change, you won't love or need me; Down deep I know you don't really care about me because knowing me why would you; I wish you knew how much I need you and your recognition.*

All of these thoughts, feelings, emotions, beliefs, and behaviors make others feel guilty in some way or another. This play on guilt may cause others to avoid the Poor Me type of individual. This avoidance only plays into the Poor Me's insecurities and creates further feelings of alienation.

The matching dramas most affected by the Poor Me are the Intimidator and the Interrogator. To the Intimidator, the Poor Me has feelings and beliefs that the Intimidator wants to control him. This victim drama is suppose to infuse a feeling of guilt into the thoughts and feelings of the Intimidator.

To the Interrogator there is an attempt by the Poor Me to create a feeling of guilt by sending the indirect message that the Interrogator is so self-centered and that he cares about nobody but himself. These matching dramas of the Poor Me only play into his own insecurities.

As a Life Coach, you will want to listen for these subtle clues and signals. They will be unknowingly revealed by your client in each of the dramas. Understanding these control dramas and their outer behavior as well as recognizing the verbal expressions of their inner struggle can be of great benefit.

It becomes very important to know how to listen for the phrases of his inner struggle. This will give you valuable insight into his deep-seated issues. Knowing and understanding these subconscious behaviors, signals, and phrases will help you to focus on the issues which he may be unaware on a conscious level.

Rather than working on the conscious level with what you, the Life Coach, are told about his symptoms and complaints, you will now have information based in his subconscious programming. Armed with this information, you will be better equipped to help him resolve his issues. In most cases, his issues were indirectly programmed into his subconscious as far back as childhood.

Keep in mind, the more information you have, the better you will be able to help your client. It's better to listen, really listen, rather than waiting to talk or trying to quickly to solve a long-term behavior or emotional problem. Seldom are the players of these Control Dramas aware of this "game" they are playing.

Behavior Patterns

Life – You – Stuff – Self Esteem

I like to refer to this tool as Stuff because of the hidden factors involved in behavioral issues. Behavior patterns can be very subtle. In fact, they may even seem natural. However, these patterns can create chaos in our lives and we may not even be aware they exist.

These patterns can cause us to lose our relationships, our jobs, our self-esteem and confidence. They can even affect our finances. The roots of these patterns can go deep into our past, stemming from negative past experiences, as well as positive past experiences. They can be caused by being treated like a little prince or princess where we could do no wrong, or they could be caused by neglect and abuse.

No matter the cause, deep within our subconscious mind, we create coping skills which may or may not work for our betterment, especially as we get older. Understanding our Behavior Patterns and how they affect our self-esteem and our ability to reach our goals is vital. These patterns can begin long before puberty and, many times, they are written off as "this is just a phase that he or she is going through."

The problem we have here is these patterns seem to build on one another, thus creating other patterns. Some of these patterns are viewed as unacceptable, while others are viewed as normal and acceptable, since we make excuses for ourselves. Not only do we make excuses for ourselves, but we make them for others. Our parents, family, loved ones, and friends may make excuses for us as well.

Let's begin with the unacceptable behaviors. We may start to smoke in order to deal with stress or just to fit in with what we consider the "in crowd." We may actually believe that it makes us look macho or sexy or cool, when in reality we are using it to cope with some issue which we are not prepared for or able to recognize.

Another is the use of alcohol. As issues continue to build and we do not know how to handle them, we continue to

Behavior Patterns

Unacceptable Behaviors		Acceptable Behaviors
Smoke	Life	Yell
Drink	You	Sleep
Drugs	**Behavior Patterns**	Depressed
Gamble	Stuff	Shop
Lie	Self-Esteem	Eat
		Party
		Work

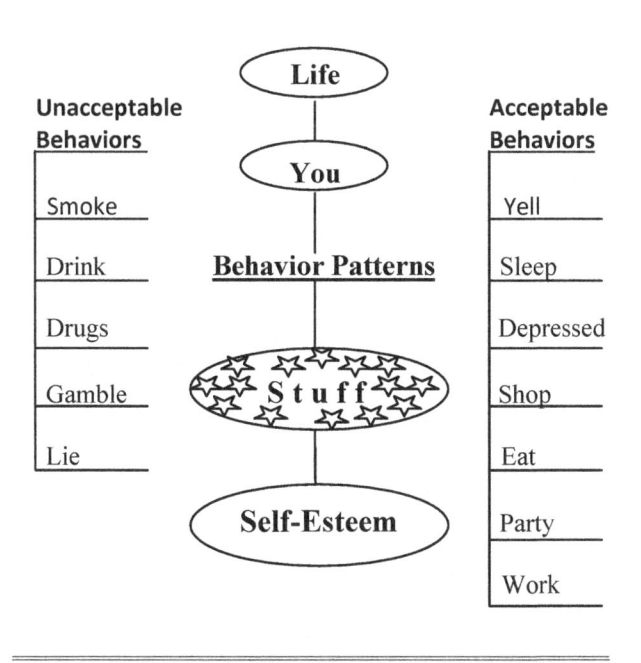

Repressed and suppressed "Stuff" from the past can cause all types of **Behavior Patterns** in the present. Some of these **Behavior Patterns** may be acceptable or tolerated and supported by a myriad of excuses while other **Behavior Patterns** done in excess are deemed unacceptable.

self-medicate, not only the use of nicotine but we begin to use alcohol as well.

Alcohol is readily available and somewhat easy to obtain. It's not long until we move to the next negative behavior, drugs.

Whether its prescription drugs or marijuana or a host of other drugs that we are able to obtain, we step up our self-medication. Rather than find a way to resolve the stressors that we are faced with, we just add another behavior or habit. We may actually believe there is no solution or we may not be aware that a problem exists.

It's not long until we find our next escape, gambling. It can be as innocent as bingo, playing the lottery, or losing your entire paycheck on the blackjack table. It's still a behavior that we use to cope with something on some level, but again we are not addressing the problem.

I call these hidden stressors "STUFF": stuff from our past; stuff at work; stuff in our relationships with spouses, children, parents; stuff with finances; and the list goes on and on. The problem is, more often than not, the symptoms are being treated rather than the real issues.

These issues are usually hidden deep within the subconscious and are only revealed through behavior patterns, organic language, paralanguage, and body language. It's easier to smoke a cigarette, have a cocktail, take a pill, or create a diversion by gambling than it is to deal with what is really bothering us.

The list of acceptable behaviors seems to be endless. A few examples of these behaviors that we use to cope are watching television, sleeping, being depressed, yelling, crying, shopping, overeating, overworking. Some of the excuses are, they make me angry, I like the taste of food, I'm tired all the time, everything bad always happens to me.

Whatever the excuse, rather than take responsibility and go inside to find the root cause of the behavior, we unknowingly compound the negative habits. Instead of reframing the perceived negative experience to make it a positive, we create these behavioral diversions. We continue finding ways of numbing ourselves down to the issues that dwell within us.

Down deep below all of this "STUFF" dwells our self-esteem, covered and polluted by the symptoms of our acceptable and unacceptable behavioral patterns. It is my personal experience that you must go inside and seek out these issues, own them and all of their parts, then reframe

them. Until you do, they will continue to haunt you and create negative outcomes in your life.
(Refer to Reframing)

This process requires a great deal of soul searching. At this point you can begin to clear out the "STUFF," which means, work on the real problems and issues. You must shift attention away from the symptoms that seem to be ever-present.

During the reframing process, you will begin experiencing a feeling of empowerment with a new view of your past and present situations. Again, these symptoms are the acceptable and the unacceptable behaviors which you have created to cope with underlying issues.

As your self-esteem and self-confidence begin to improve, it will motivate you to continue your inner journey. For many, this process is the most difficult challenge of their life. However, it is also the most rewarding. To reach a point where you have the self-esteem and confidence, not questioning your actions, your behaviors, or your decisions can be very rewarding.

As a Life Coach, being able to identify the Behavior Patterns of your client can be vital. To focus and hone in on real issues is a skill/tool well worth having in your tool chest. Your ability to assess and make the connection between the "stuff" from the past and the Behavioral Patterns expressed in their everyday life will serve both you and your client well.

(Refer to the illustration in this chapter)

One of my team of first responders when I begin seeing a new client is the Behavior Patterns process. I may not use it during the first few sessions; however, I will normally use it within the first three or four. Of course, it depends on the individual and his issues, as to which tools I will use and in what order.

As the Life Coach and the client work on identifying the root cause of a Behavior Pattern and reframe it, as well as other attached issues, the behavior will begin to diminish. It has been my experience that as those other issues attached to the behavior are resolved; the behavior stemming from them will change or simply fade away.

The Behavior Patterns tool is an excellent way to help the client reflect back to a time in his life when certain behaviors started. He then can explore who was involved in his life and what may have led up to the beginning of a certain behavior. It does not necessarily have to be a particular person or event.

The client may have developed a defiant attitude early on and his problems may have developed from his behavior. Consequently, his parents and others involved in rearing him may not have known how to handle such behavior in a positive manner, thus causing more negative behaviors. If this is the case, the Life Coach may explore ways to alter that particular trait.

Control / Approval

I have used, with great success, the Want of Control/ Want of Approval tool for many years as another one of my first responder tools in a variety of issues. It is an excellent exercise that can be used for: releasing anger, resentment issues, relationship issues, controlling problems, and workplace issues.

This is one of my main go-to tools both personally and professionally. It is an enormous help when working with fear and anger. While fear and anger play a major role in all of our lives on some level, it is important to have a way to combat them.

When using this tool, the Life Coach assists the client in separating and breaking down negative thoughts and feelings into one of two categories. By using the tool, "The Want of Control or The Want of Approval," the individual can simplify a very complex series of emotions or feelings. The client may think or feel that these complex feelings and emotions cannot be altered.

As the emotions and feelings are separated from one another, they then can be approached one at a time. In the beginning it will seem very difficult to go through the process. It gets easier and easier until finally it practically works automatically.

Before going through this releasing exercise, it is important the individual become sincere and emotionally involved. When using this tool, make sure the individual's voice is centered because centering the voice will make the process more effective. To become emotionally involved we must first work with the voice to ensure that the voice is resonating from the heart chakra.

It is important to know from where the voice is resonating. The release must come from the heart, and not the head. In order for this to happen, the voice may need to be moved. Keep in mind, the emotional pain the client is experiencing is of the heart.

It has been my experience that before the individual came to me, that he had spent a lot of time reasoning and trying to figure out in his head how to resolve the problem. Chances are he will need help getting from his head back to his heart. This is accomplished by moving the voice.

To this point, I have never had anyone who was aware this shift from the heart to the head had taken place, nor were they aware their voice had moved. The movement of the voice is very slow and subtle. Even though the voice moves off-center the emotional pain remains in the heart; herein lies part of the problem.
(Refer to Voice)

The next issue we must deal with before going through the process of releasing "The Want of Control or The Want of Approval," is taking ownership of the problem. It is almost impossible to get rid of something you do not own. As long as you blame someone or something else for your unhappiness, they (or it) own the problem.

Without ownership, the individual can't do anything about the emotional pain he is experiencing, he is stuck. So the first thing is to find a way to take ownership of the issue.

This will require a little acceptance of certain feelings on the part of the client.

(Refer to Owning the Problem)

Before we actually start the exercise, I inform my client he only has two choices from which to name what he is feeling: The Want of Control or The Want of Approval. He must select from these two choices only. If he wants both control and approval, we must go through the process separately for each.

Normally, I will have the Want of Control and Want of Approval written on the board so that he can refer to the choices. I will ask him what he thinks the key word is at this point. The key word is "want." When you want control you do not have it. "You want it." When you have control, you do not want it because "You already have it."

Before we actually go through the Want of Control or the Want of Approval process I explain that we really can't control another person. We may coerce them or manipulate them in some way, but we can't control them. So to even try is fruitless; however, it seems we still make an attempt.

As for getting approval, I explain that if someone doesn't like or approve of you, it is very difficult to change how they feel. You can give them money or any other type of gift and they will still tell a friend, "That was a nice gesture for such a jerk." What is of value here is how "you" feel about "you."

I begin the process by asking the individual to tell me about the last time he was angry at someone or about something. When he answers, I ask, "How does that make you feel?" I have heard answers ranging from; "it makes me feel like screaming, sick to my stomach, angry all over, it hurts my heart," to, "I feel like beating the crap out of him."

I then ask him to touch where he feels this feeling is in his body. At this point I say, "Now that you've indentified the feeling let's name it." This is where we begin to separate the feeling from the emotion. What he is feeling and where he is feeling it is much different from emotionally expressing what he would like to do about that feeling.

This is when he will choose between the Want of Control and the Want of Approval. Again, he can "choose" only one. To assist the client, the Life Coach must be prepared to give a few simple examples of control and approval without making the choice for him.

If you want someone to do something, or do something different, or do it differently, then it is Control. Should you want someone to accept you for the way you are, or what you are doing, or how you are doing it, then you are seeking Approval. Explaining this to the client will help him differentiate between the two as he makes his choice.

After we have named the feeling (Want of Control), I then ask, "Would you be willing to accept this angry want of control feeling that you have in your body?" This is the point where they actually begin to own the feeling. Seldom has anyone accepted that angry want of control feeling the first time they are asked.

Most of the time the answer is, "No, I'm not willing to accept it, I don't want it, I don't like it." I then explain to them they have it, it's inside of them, it's been there for an extended period of time, you might as well accept it. At this point I may refer back to the analogy that I used about the Ferrari in the chapter on "Owning the Problem." I may also use a few other analogies. *(Refer to Owning the Problem)*

I try not to tell them they must own it before we can go any further. It's always better if they are led to the answer and discover it on their own. It is well worth the extra time you spend helping them to realize that before they can get rid of the feeling, they must accept and own it. The Life Coach may have to get a little creative at this point with examples.

After they understand, agree, and accept this angry feeling which they have now named the Want of Control (or Want of Approval), I immediately ask them, "Would you like to get rid of it?" Remember, only work with one at a time, either control or approval. I've never had anyone tell me "NO" they would not accept the feeling after realizing what is taking place.

Here is where the release begins. I have them stand up, I place the palm of their right hand over their heart chakra, I place my hand over their hand, and I place my left hand directly opposite on their back. To make sure their voice is resonating through their heart chakra, I will ask them a few questions like their address or where they were born or the name of their family members.

I ask them to be sincere and answer the questions from the heart. It is very important their voice resonates through their hand and into yours. This is getting them out of their head and into their heart. If it doesn't resonate through your hands, go back and work on moving the voice.
(Refer to Voice)

Once we have their voice resonating through the heart charka, I ask them to close their eyes. I then repeat what has taken place up to this point. "You have identified your angry feeling. You have named that angry feeling the Want of Control. You have owned that feeling by accepting it." I then asked you if you would like to get rid of that feeling, and you answered "yes."

The repeating of the process and what has taken place up until present, helps them get into the "now." The repeating of the process also helps maintain continuity in the exercise. The repetition of what we have covered helps the client remember the process. This make it easier to apply to other issues.

With your eyes remaining closed and from your heart repeat after me: "I am willing….. to release….. the want to control you (Bill, Bob, Sue, Jane, Etc.)….. You go live your life….. and be the jerk that you are….. if that's working for you….. But I will no longer participate in any form….. I have chosen instead….. to set you free….. to do, say or be anything you choose….. I am willing to release you at this point….. I am willing …..to release the want to control you."

At this stage of the process I have them imagine the person standing in front of them. I ask them to imagine looking directly into the eyes of that individual (use their name). I then say, "When you are ready, simply tell them, 'I now release you (use the name).'"

Once they say they now release the person, I immediately have them repeat the following after me: "You go ahead and go on with your life….. but I will no longer participate….. it's your right to experience the grief….. that you have allowed to come into your life….. I choose not to participate anymore….. so I now release you (use the name)."

The key phrases here are "I am willing to release the want to control you" and "I now release you." It is important for your client to use the person's name or, if it is a parent, use mom or dad. The phrases that follow are what I call riffs. You will want to come up with phrases (riffs) that are appropriate for you and your client.

Many times when we get to the point of actually saying "I now release you," people begin crying. Some will stop and say, "I'm not willing to do this anymore." This means they are unwilling to let go of the pain and misery at this time. They may have been holding onto the pain for many years or most of their life so it is familiar. We simply stop and discuss what their issues are with releasing this individual.

After we work through the issues, which may take a few sessions more or less, we then go back and begin the process again. When the release actually takes place, it will be followed by a light feeling and/or in most cases a very deep sigh. The release may also be described as feeling like a heavy weight has been lifted.

The problem that is most encountered in this process is getting the voice to resonate through the heart chakra. This may be accomplished by using the analogies in the chapter on Voice. The next is getting them to accept what they are feeling.

Sometimes, I will go through the process before attempting to move the voice so that the individual knows what to expect, kind of a trial run. During this trial run I'll point out where their voice is resonating from and explain to them that the release must come from the heart, not the head.

Self-Esteem

Trust, Honesty, Responsibility, Integrity, Listen to Your Inner Voice, Listen to Your Emotions, Never Hurt Self or Others. These are the components and steps of self-esteem that we will be discussing in this chapter. I consider these components the main players of self-esteem.

Self-Esteem plays a major role in the journey to self-discovery. I have narrowed down the steps that I have used on my own journey and I use these steps when working with others. Self-Esteem and Self-Confidence go hand in hand. To me it's about embarking upon a spiritual journey into self. I believe it to be the most sacred life-changing journey one will ever experience.

When working with my clients on self-esteem, I begin by listening to their issues. During this part of the session I am paying very close attention to changes in their body language, facial expressions, breaks in their voice, and any other signals or clues I may observe. I may interrupt them at any given moment and say, "Let's freeze frame that," because they have said something I think is significant having to do with their self-esteem.

At this time, I will begin to do "board talk" and will write the seven steps to self-esteem on the white board one at a time. I explain and give examples of how each step is used and how it works. I will also include things they have just told me or something I picked up during the pre-talk so it is personalized.

Most of the time I will use their own words and repeat back to them what they just said, verbatim. I also ask them questions, such as, what they meant by that remark and what changes they would have to make in order to achieve each step as I write them on the white board.

Once we have gone over all the steps thoroughly, I then do what I call "locking it in." Here is where I do hypnosis with them. I will do an induction (relaxation). While they are in hypnosis I will go over everything we had covered during the waking state (waking hypnosis or pre-talk).

Most of the time I will construct a metaphor using information gathered during the pre-talk and what we covered during the board talk part of the session. Keep in mind, when developing a metaphor or simply locking in what has been covered during the session, repetition is very important.
(Refer to my book: The Art & Structure of Metaphor in Hypnosis)

Trust

Trust is my first component of Self-Esteem. This is not a matter of can you trust me or can I trust you or someone else. It is a matter of trusting yourself enough to go inside and take a look around at who you are, what you are about, how you came to be the way you are. It also includes why you think the way you think and believe the things you believe. It is a time to ask yourself: "Are these beliefs, attitudes, and behaviors working for me?"

Honesty

Honesty is the second component of Self-Esteem. You must trust yourself enough to go inside take a look around and be totally and completely honest with yourself. This does not mean go inside, take a look around, and blame or make excuses for yourself. It is a time to begin taking responsibility.

This is the time to own who you have become. It is a matter of being honest about what is working and what is not working in your life. This is a time to explore your beliefs. Being honest with yourself includes all of the positives you are as well as the negatives. It is a time of growth.

Responsibility

Responsibility is our next component on the journey to Self-Esteem. As you trust yourself enough to go inside, take a look around and be totally and completely honest with yourself; then you must respond to your discoveries. You must respond in a positive manner and take responsibility.

Do something about your issues; take some type of corrective action. Make the changes that need to be made for you to find balance in your life. Taking responsibility may require changing beliefs and behaviors you have held for many years.

Make no excuses because it may require looking at yourself, owning your own issues, and doing something about them, no matter how difficult or trying things may appear. In this process, you must really want to, not wish to, not like to, but really want to make your life better for yourself and those around you.
(Refer to Reframing)

Integrity

Integrity will be our next component of Self-Esteem. It's time to ask yourself what integrity means to you, from you, and for you. For me, it meant a spontaneous, honest, responsible interaction with my reality, meaning, am I happy? Have I achieved the things I wanted in my life or have I at least tried my best?

Here integrity means more than doing what you say you will do or not doing what you say you won't do. These basic fundamentals of integrity are easy to say, but for many not so easy to accomplish. I have been asked many times, how in the world do you know what to do or what action to take? My response involves the next three steps to Self-Esteem.

Most of us are programmed to think and believe in the "social norm." The social norm may not work for some people because of a variety of reasons. To challenge what we were taught and who taught it to us takes a bit of soul-searching and a true quest for our own personal truth.

Questions that may come to mind may include: Do I believe in God or a higher power? If so, why? How did I come to take on this belief? Why am I here on this earth? Am I doing what I came here to do? If so, why? If not, then why not? Who taught me all of this and did it work for them or were they just passing on, without question what they were taught?

Integrity means being true to self. It means discovering why you believe what you believe and do what you do. It means changing from old programs that no longer work to ones that will. It means going beyond the norm and

embarking upon a spiritual journey into self and discovering and living to your full potential.
(Refer to Self-Esteem)

Inner Voice

Our next component of Self-Esteem is Inner Voice. Listen to your Inner Voice, without bias. This can be a very difficult task for those individuals who sit quietly and seem to hear many voices (internal chatter). For me this step involved learning to meditate. As I sat quietly and cleared my mind, slowly in the beginning, the chatter began to fade.

I learned to trust myself more, be honest with myself, and take responsibility for my own happiness and behaviors. Finally, there was only one voice left which has guided me for many years without confusion or doubt. This required patience and determination.

I have a very close friend who is an accountant. One day in a meeting she said that even though she may have all of the facts in front of her and they certainly make sense she is unable to "pull the trigger" and make the final decision and take action on a project. She said to me, "It seems you have no problem making that decision no matter the consequences."

My reply was, "I'm not afraid to fail because I do not look at not accomplishing my desired outcome as failure. I view it as a learning experience." I told her a long time ago I had embarked upon a process, a spiritual journey, if you will. It led me to believe in myself.

Even if things do not go as planned, I am still led by that Inner Voice, that inner guide. However, you must first get in touch with your higher self. It helps you conquer all: fears, addictions, feelings of being disconnected, abuse, lost, low to no Self-Esteem, and the list is endless.

Your inner voice will not argue with you, it will not seek you out, it will not insist. It just waits for you. It waits for you to reach a time in your life when you seek out answers and ask of yourself rather than others.

Hypnosis played a major role in my life. It helped me cut through the obstacles and resolve many issues which may have taken years to accomplish and reframe. The desire to find answers and a willingness to challenge my beliefs played a major role in the process.

Emotions

Emotions are our next component of Self-Esteem. Learn to listen to your emotions. It seems as though very few people appear to have control of their emotions. In fact, they let their raw emotions control them and how they act or react to both positive and negative situations.

As you learn to listen to your Inner Voice and your Emotions, they will tell you what you need to do to take charge of your emotional self. In general this will put you more in charge of your life. This means taking responsibility for your decisions no matter the outcome.

Never Hurt Self or Others

Never hurt yourself or others is the final step in this exercise. I find it amazing how many people when making a mistake say negative and derogatory things about themselves. It seems they pick up where other people who have verbally abused them in the past had left off.

Here in this part of the process the Life Coach may want to make a few suggestions to the client. This is an excellent starting point for change. Now is a good starting time to stop saying anything negative or derogatory about yourself ever again, despite what may happen.

I recommend to my clients they choose a private setting, look themselves in the mirror, right into their pupils, and say, "I forgive you. I love you and forgive you for whatever you may have done in the past. I promise you to stop this negative behavior toward myself." If a particular past behavior is brothering the client, have him name the issue when forgiving himself.

I suggest they put their hand over their heart chakra and say to themselves, "I love you and I am going to be good to you and I am going to take care of you, mentally, physically, psychologically, and emotionally from now on for the rest of my life." I have been told by several clients this is a very difficult assignment. I reassure them it gets much easier when they do it often.

As I bring the session to a close, I suggest to my client to write a love letter or a love poem to their inner child. I also have them bring it with them and read it during their next session. This process helps in clearing up any misconceptions they may have about the process. Reading it aloud in front of me has a deeper subconscious impact.

Here is an example of how I use hypnosis to "lock in" what I have covered during the Self-Esteem session. Notice the repetition and the different ways it is done. You may want to use your own induction. If, as a Life Coach, you do not use hypnosis, you can have your client close their eyes, take a moment and relax, and then slowly read the script to them.

The Life Coach will want to begin this metaphor with his own induction or use the one provided here. This induction is also used in the Tree Metaphor. You will then work the induction into the script while using information gathered during the pre-talk. The induction is quite lengthy; however, it is one I prefer and it seems to produce the best effect and results.

Hypnosis script

Take a moment and relax..... Now just take a deep breath through your nose and hold it a few moments..... Now release the breath through your mouth..... Take another deep breath through your nose hold it a few moments..... and now release it through your mouth..... Now take another deep breath through your nose..... Hold it..... Hold it..... Now release it through your mouth and just let your eyes go closed.

Now just begin to relax your eyes..... Relax the fronts of your eyes..... relax the sides of your eyes..... and relax the backs of your eyes..... Begin now to relax all of the tissue around your eyes..... Let it become soft and pliable..... easy and gentle..... cool and comfortable..... so very relaxed..... That all of the muscles around your eyes..... throughout your face, scalp, and neck..... just lets go as you move deeper and deeper..... into a total and complete state of relaxation.

Relax your eyes just as though you were asleep now..... relax your eyes just as though you (are) asleep now..... Relax your eyes till they just won't work now..... relax your eyes till they just..... won't..... work now..... When you are sure..... when you are absolutely sure now..... your eyes just won't work now..... very gently test them.

Now let that relaxed feeling fall down through your face and neck..... Let it move down into your chest..... let it tumble down through your abdomen, relaxing everything in its path..... Let it move down through your groin, down through your thighs, your knees, down through your calves, through your ankles, into your feet and right out the bottom of your feet.

Now..... experience this relaxation throughout your entire body..... through every muscle in your body..... through every blood vessel in your body..... through every nerve ending..... all the way down to the bone marrow.

As you experience this relaxation taking place..... Let your mind begin to drift..... let your thoughts begin to wonder about new ways..... and new things and new attitudes..... new behaviors..... Let your mind begin to drift to other places..... Imagine your thoughts beginning to wonder about what it would be like..... if you..... "Now....." take a new look at the way you think..... at the way you feel..... and the way you behave.

And you realize..... that it's "Now....." time to make changes..... and you wonder about what those changes might be..... what would be the benefits to you?..... What would be the benefits to you..... if you..... "Now....." let your thoughts begin to shift..... to change..... to take on a new perspective?

And you just imagine with your mind drifting..... and your thoughts wondering..... about this new perspective..... Imagine if you took some time..... you took some time alone to do some thinking..... to restructure..... to prioritize..... not only your life..... but the way you think..... and the way you feel about life..... and what you came here on this earth to do.

Imagine now..... how good it feels to have embarked upon this spiritual journey into self..... A journey of self-discovery..... just let yourself feel how good it feels..... to trust yourself..... trust yourself enough to embark upon this spiritual journey..... to go inside and take a look around..... Feel how good it feels to trust yourself enough..... to go inside of yourself..... and take a look around..... at who you are..... and the changes that need to be made..... to bring true happiness into your life.

Think how sacred it is..... to trust yourself enough to go inside..... take a look around..... and be honest with yourself..... about who you were..... who you are..... and who you're becoming..... Honesty..... being honest with yourself about all of the positives you are..... and all the positive things you have accomplished..... Just like trust is a quality of self-esteem..... so is honesty a quality of self-esteem.

Trust builds self-confidence..... and honesty builds confidence..... To trust yourself enough to be honest with yourself..... and then do something..... about the changes..... that must be made now..... is being responsible..... Responsibility is a quality of self esteem..... and the steps to get there..... are the qualities of being there..... and the qualities of being there are the steps to get there.

You..... here..... now..... you..... in this deep state of self-actualization..... mind..... body..... spirit..... thoughts..... feelings..... emotions..... wants..... needs..... desires..... working together with your conscious..... your subconscious..... and your unconscious to bring about changes in the way you think..... in the way you feel..... and the way you behave.

These changes are good..... because they are from your spiritual self..... your higher self..... your esoteric self..... Call it what you may..... these changes are from you, to you, for you, of you, by you..... this is good..... of course these changes are good..... because these changes are from your higher self.

Responsibility..... to actually take action..... and respond to those areas of your life..... where changes need to be made..... is a part of self-esteem..... To trust yourself enough to be honest with yourself..... and now take responsibility..... and make the changes..... you now..... must make..... to bring peace, harmony, tranquility and balance into your life..... is actually a form of integrity..... Self-integrity.

Integrity is a quality of self-esteem..... Integrity..... that honest responsible interaction with your reality..... doing what you say you are going to do..... and not doing what you say you are not going to do..... Trusting yourself..... being honest with yourself..... being responsible..... are all qualities of self-esteem..... Listening to your inner voice..... is a quality of self-esteem.

Listening to your inner voice..... that part of you that knows..... that part of you that leads and guides you..... but only when you are ready to listen..... only when you are ready to tune in to it..... And now..... you have reached a point in your life..... that you are ready..... You are ready to listen..... you..... are ready to make changes..... changes..... in the way you think..... changes..... in the way you feel..... changes..... in the way you behave.

You..... now..... realize that it's time..... in fact it's way past time..... to listen to your emotions..... Your emotions will let you know..... what change you now must make..... all you have to do is..... now..... listen to your emotions..... listen through your feelings..... watch through your actions and behaviors..... It's now..... time to make changes..... it's now..... time to make the changes for your own well-being..... your own self-esteem..... for your own betterment.

Self-esteem..... means no more derogatory remarks..... towards yourself or others..... Self-esteem..... means never hurt yourself or others..... From this time forward..... you find deep within you….. there is a feeling of compassion….. for yourself and others….. a feeling of peace, harmony and tranquility….. as you now….. begin to live and experience….. what it's really like….. to have and live the qualities of self-esteem.

Trust….. trust yourself enough to go inside and be honest with yourself….. To be responsible for your actions….. your feelings….. your emotions….. to have the integrity….. to make the changes that it takes….. to bring peace, and balance into your life….. Trusting yourself enough….. to be honest with yourself….. to be responsible….. to have the integrity to listen to your inner voice….. to truly lead and guide you in your life.

It's now time….. to listen to your emotions….. so you can easily identify….. those areas where changes must be made….. and now….. realize it's time to stop hurting yourself and others….. It's time to make the changes….. it's time to make the changes….. mind….. body….. spirit….. working in harmony….. with your conscious….. your subconscious….. your thoughts….. your feelings….. your emotions….. to bring about the changes that are taking place at this very moment…..

Deep within you..... Feel it..... Feel it..... Feel how good it feels..... to feel good..... about feeling good..... about feeling good about yourself..... and these changes..... that are taking place..... deep within you at this very moment..... changes that will continue..... for the rest of your life..... this is good..... this is very good for your own personal well-being.

I'm going to count from one to five, when I say five and only when I say five and snap my fingers will you open your eyes feeling good in every way. Begin here to use your count-out procedure. Be sure to include several post-hypnotic suggestions during your count-out.

Purpose

One of the major factors involved in making changes in life has to do with Purpose. To find your Purpose requires you to embark upon a journey into self. I find it amazing the number of individuals who seem to wander through life without Purpose.
(Refer to Self-Esteem)

As we begin to get deeper into the client's issues, I ask a series of, what I consider to be, though-provoking questions. These include the following: "What is your purpose in life?" "Why do you think you are here on this earth?" "Are you doing what you came here to do?"

In many cases these questions help shift attention from petty issues to those more profound. Those petty issues then can be addressed with a fresh approach. When put in a new context many of those issues seem unimportant.

This is the beginning of getting the client unstuck from a way of thinking which is not working.

I have asked these questions to people of ages from teens to people in their eighties. I could count on one hand those individuals who replied, "Yes I do know my purpose." In fact, over the years, I have asked these questions of people who came to me for a variety of reasons. These issues include weight loss, depression, anxiety, anger, addiction, feelings of emptiness, relationship issues. None of these individuals said they knew their Purpose.

Recently, a woman came to me who wanted to lose one hundred pounds. After we talked for a while and I gathered the routine information, I asked her, "What is your purpose?" This question was a complete shift away from her complaints. After a moment of contemplation she replied, "I really don't have a purpose, I never really thought about it. What does that have to do with my weight problem?"

My response to her was, "Then why not eat? Why do you want to lose weight?" Over the years I've had several people ask me what is their Purpose. Of course, I responded, "It's up to you to go within and discover your own purpose. I can help you, but I can't do it for you."

In my opinion, without Purpose you basically just wander through life being a victim of circumstance. As most of us know, it is not what happens to you but how you handle what happens. This may require changing a way of thinking or believing to achieve more positive outcomes.

In the beginning, we may be unaware of our Purpose due to circumstances: our young age, living conditions, being a parent, caring for someone, college, or handling the many situations we encounter in life. At the time, dealing with these may be one of our goals. It has been my experience that at some point a deeper and more spiritual question about Purpose presents itself.

As time passes and we reach a certain stage in our lives when it seems we've "been there, done that," and we still feel unfulfilled, the big questions present themselves. We begin to ask more deeper and spiritual questions of ourselves or possibly ponder the essence of life.

When it comes to using the Purpose tool, the task of the Life Coach is to first of all, call upon his listening skills. Really listen to the deeper meaning of what the client is saying. Perhaps in the beginning his Purpose might be to find his Purpose. This usually requires a bit of soul-searching.

Once he has established or discovered his Purpose, he then begins to set his goals and aspirations. The client's discovery of his Purpose will assist the Life Coach in helping him resolve many issues that he may be struggling with on a daily basis. This brings us to consistency of Purpose.

Consistency of Purpose

Everything you do either helps or hurts: "Nothing is Neutral." Consistency of Purpose is where you focus all of your energy in achieving those goals of your Purpose. It is my belief that everything you do either helps or hurts your Purpose; nothing is neutral.

If, within your Purpose, a goal is to repair or make your relationships better, then before you say or do anything, ask yourself, "Will what I'm about to say or do help or hurt my Purpose?" As purpose becomes the focus, it is likely to contain many goals.

It will certainly require you to set priorities in order to achieve those goals. This will require a plan. I suggest making a minimum of a ten-year plan. Having a ten-year plan allows for many unforeseen contingencies which may occur while working to achieve those goals. This allows for time to take care of unexpected events and still remain on course.
(Refer to Ten-Year Plan)

I have found for myself, and heard from others as well, when Purpose is established and goals and priorities are set, many petty issues in life begin to fade away because the main focus is then to work diligently toward those goals and aspirations.

As people find their Purpose there is a calmness that seems to come over them. They become more focused and relationships become better, not only in their private life but their public life as well. Many of those petty issues that bothered them in the past are quickly resolved or simply no longer seem important.

Above all, the first step is, You have to want to. Really Want To, Not like to, Not wish to, But Really Want To make the changes that will put you in control of your thoughts, feelings, and emotions. Thus putting you more in control of your life.

(Refer to Owning the Problem)

Motivation and Focus

Often I am asked, "How do you get on path? How do you know where to start when you've been off-track for so long?" Years ago my younger brother came to talk to me about being depressed. He stated that it seems that he was unable to make anything of his life.

As I listened, he went on to say that he just kept going back and forth between making plans and not following through. He said he just couldn't make a plan and stick with it or stay motivated. I told him I didn't have that problem. He quickly replied, "Yes we know. You just hit the ground running and didn't look back. How do you do it?"

As we continued to talk, I began to explain to him how I escaped many of the pitfalls he had mentioned; however, I had my own issues to overcome. I went on to say, "As you know I left home very early in my teens. For some unknown reason I also realized during that time that if I didn't make 'It' happen, 'It' wasn't going to happen. No one in the family seemed to care what I did or what would become of me."

I told him even when I was very young I had dreams of living life on my terms. This meant I would have to do things I didn't necessarily want to do but needed to in order to fulfill those dreams. Some of those things included taking a look at what I had come to believe and why I believed them to be true. I needed to learn how to recognize and change negative thoughts and behaviors in all areas of my life. Another was to go back to school and educate myself.

I continued explaining how I "hit the ground running and didn't look back." I told him I had come to some important realizations very early in my teens. I think it was because of the way I had been treated by his father, my stepfather. There was no way I would let my stepfather make me a victim nor would I use him as an excuse for my shortcomings.

First of all, to achieve my dreams, I had to truly be honest with myself and take responsibility for my actions and behaviors. I realized I had to have "Purpose" and with that purpose I must have Consistency of Purpose. This required me to make a plan, a ten-year plan, put it in writing, keep it up dated and follow it no matter how difficult. I admitted to him this was no easy task, especially in the beginning when I was young, but it needed to be done.

I put on the whiteboard one of the many illustrations we would cover in the coming weeks. This particular illustration is one of the formulas I use to stay on track. I believe it helped me to avoid a host of issues, including the boredom and depression which my brother had been struggling with for years.

It even helped during those times in college when I became frustrated while attempting to learn something I did not understand. I used it when going through other difficult times in my life. I simply took a step back and refocused on my Purpose.

(Refer to Reframing)

Motivation and Focus

Behaviors

Good			Bad
Work hard	→	→	Miss work
Go to school	←	←	Quit school
Save money	→	→	Spend money
Nice person	←	←	Jerk

⬇

Meditation

What Do I Want
  To be successful
  To be independent
  Nobody tell me what to do

Must Work for Myself and Stay Focused

↳

Must be a
  Self-starter
  Self-motivator
Must Educate Myself

Realized Success Has Two Categories
  Money (The language of the Earth)
  Spirituality (The language of the Universe)

Over the years I have used meditation to stay focused and on course to my **Purpose** rather than the back and forth between the "Good and Bad" or "Positive and Negative" behaviors.

The process goes as follows:

I write on the board what I consider important for me to stay on Purpose. The Life Coach will want to listen to the client and obtain what is important to him and help determine his Purpose. This may take several sessions and the use of many tools.

For me, work, education, independence, and how I feel about myself have always been very important, so I begin with these as examples. I said to my brother, "If you do not like your work, either learn to like it or change your work. This change could be risky or require going to school for a new career. I didn't say it was going to be easy.

It can be very easy to become burnt out, get lazy, or simply take your job for granted. During the burnt-out stage there is a tendency to drop school, spend your savings, and basically become depressed and grouchy." He quickly agreed with me and said, "That is exactly what I've been doing."

Without a job you will be unable to cover your expenses, and thus experience a loss of independence. After slipping over to the negative or "bad side," it's not long until you realize things are not working for you, so you start trying to "get it back together again." He replied, "You're right you just described me again."

Without purpose and a plan, again, you soon begin to slip over to the negative side and then the cycle continues. This is a crucial point in the process. Once the Purpose is determined you then must find what needs to be done to achieve your Purpose. You now replace the negative thoughts and behaviors with your Purpose as shown in the illustration.

When replacing a negative behavior with a positive, it will feel strange in the beginning. However, the more the "strange positive" is practiced the more it becomes the norm. At some point the "strange positive" will replace the negative "norm" behavior and become the norm. Then when the old negative behavior is experienced it becomes the "strange negative" feeling and will be avoided.

Keep in mind, what success means to one person can be different for another. It is up to the individual to determine what is important to him. The Life Coach may give examples to show the process as illustrated here, however, it still remains the client's responsibility to make his own determination.

The next step is to make a realistic plan to achieve the desired outcome. It is important to discuss what it takes to stay on track. The plan must be in writing and looked at every day. I suggest putting it on the bedroom wall where it can be seen the first thing in the morning and the last thing before sleep.

Meditation is what I have used over the years to keep my focus, especially during difficult times. I sit in front of my plan during my meditation. This helps imprint my Purpose into my subconscious, so after a while it becomes a natural part of my thinking and behavior. It may be difficult in the beginning for some individuals to clear their mind.

One of the objectives of meditation is to help the individual get into the "Now" where changes can take place. Most of us do not live in the "Now." We are too worried about what we didn't get done yesterday and what we have to do tomorrow. This makes it difficult to ever truly experience what it is like to be in the "Now."

Keep in mind there is no yesterday. It's gone forever; we only have a selective memory of yesterday. Unfortunately, we have a tendency to focus on the unpleasant and negative experiences. For many of us, there is no tomorrow; there is only hope for tomorrow. To make changes we must get into the "Now."

This meditation has two main parts for making changes. The first part of the meditation helps the individual clear his mind and get into the "Now." The second is the undirected part which helps reprogram negative thoughts and behaviors.

This is where the Purpose which has been written into a plan comes into play. Place the plan on the wall in front of you close enough so it can easily be read. Sit comfortably and focus on the details of the plan.

You will be opening and closing your eyes during the meditation. The opening and closing of the eyes is used as a deepening technique in hypnosis. It also lets you change your focus to different topics as you proceed through the meditation. Each time you open your eyes, you may find a different detail that catches your attention and shifts your thoughts. Keep in mind; meditation and self-hypnosis are one and the same.

I use the following meditation in conjunction with many of the tools and exercises I teach my clients. I find it an excellent exercise for stilling/clearing the mind. Once this clearing is accomplished, the changes which are being worked on can take place on a subconscious level, and of course, be experienced in one's behavior.

Meditation

As you sit there focusing on the details of your plan take a couple of deep breaths through your nose and slowly release them through your mouth and let your eyes go closed.

Shift your focus to about eighteen inches above your head. Start there and do a quick relaxation. Imagine a sieve shaking back and forth as you bring it down through your body relaxing every part of your body along the way.

Now, with your eyes closed, begin thinking about yesterday in detail from the time you woke up in the morning until you went to sleep at night. Think about showering, getting dressed, making breakfast, getting the children off for the day, and basically going through your morning routine.

Think about the morning until noon, and the people you encountered and how you may have felt. Did you feel inferior, superior, angry, sad or happy? Think about what may have brought on those feelings. Think about any meetings you may have attended and what feelings may have been aroused.

Think about whom you may have had lunch with and the topics of conversation. Think about the entire afternoon in as much detail as you can remember. Don't worry if there are things you forgot. Think about everything that happened yesterday evening until you went to bed and fell asleep.

This takes care of yesterday. Keep in mind, there is no yesterday. There is only selective memory of yesterday. Yesterday is gone and will never return. However, what is remembered about yesterday can be changed.

Now shift your attention on tomorrow. Visualize waking up and going through your morning routine. Imagine going through the day finishing everything that needs to be done. This includes anything that was not completed yesterday or today.

Think about any meetings or encounters with people who may provoke positive or negative feelings. Play close attention to the ebb and flow of your changing feelings.

Think about what is going to take place throughout the evening until you retire for the night.

This takes care of tomorrow. Keep in mind, there is no tomorrow. There is only hope for tomorrow and for many of us, tomorrow will never come. Yet we must plan for tomorrow using information gained from the past.

Now focus on today and do the same as the other days. Think, in detail, from the time you woke up this morning until you are sitting there this very moment. Be sure to pay close attention to your changing feelings and emotions. At this point, you have taken care of yesterday, tomorrow and today. This gets you into the "Now."

If your head is slumped over, slowly raise it up to stare at your plan. Do not move your head around. Now open your eyes and stare at your plan. Keep them open for ten to twelve seconds, do not count, just close them when it feels like the time has passed.

Once you have closed your eyes, let whatever thoughts or memories that come to mind continue unabated. Do not censor, no matter how silly, ridiculous or serious. Let the thoughts go until they run out. This is the undirected part of the meditation. You may not consciously be aware of the connection between your thoughts and your plan.

When the thoughts or memories end, then slowly open your eyes and stare at your plan again for ten to twelve seconds. Focus on whatever part of the plan that catches your attention, then close your eyes and set your thoughts and memories free. Again, let them go unabated until they come to an end. Repeat this process three times each time you meditate.

In hypnosis, the opening and closing of the eyes is a deepening technique. Even though you may not feel as though you are going deeper, you actually are going deeper into self. Here is where many of those repressed and suppressed issues will be directly altered in an indirect manner.

After about three weeks of doing undirected meditation, you may now begin to venture into a more directed mediation using the above process. This involves writing a few words on a sticky note describing something you would like to resolve. Place the sticky note in the palm of your hand before starting your meditation.

Upon going through the preceding meditation process, open your eyes a fourth time and stare at the words on the sticky note. Then close your eyes and let your thoughts go. Try not to get too wordy; keep it short and to the point using as few words as possible to describe your issue.

You may not always have thoughts and memories or visualizations each time you open and close your eyes. It's all right. Wait a moment or two with your eyes closed and continue on with the process. Your subconscious will still be working on your changes.

Regularly mediating reinforces your plan and your changes. It also helps your subconscious to continue aligning your thoughts, feelings, emotions, and actions with your wants, needs, and desires. This, of course, helps you stay focused on achieving your "Purpose."

I suggest to my clients to meditate thirty minutes at least twice a day. For me, first thing in the morning and just before going to bed seem to work best; however, I meditate in the middle of the day as often as possible. After the first time or two it should only take thirty minutes for the entire process. I believe if you meditate every day for a month it will change your life. This certainly does not mean you stop after a month. Imagine the positive changes if you take the time for yourself and continue to meditate every day.

Own the Problem

As long as you complain and blame someone or something else for your unhappiness, anger, or misfortune, they, or it, own the problem and you are stuck with the misery. It is imperative that you take control of the problem and figure a way to own it.

Owning the Problem can be very difficult at times, especially when you see the other person as the cause. Ultimately, you are the one who must decide whether you want to play the game and maintain the pain or take ownership and disconnect. Most of us individually have had some rough times in our lives. That doesn't give us a free pass to make someone else's life unpleasant.

Once you Own the Problem, it is yours and you can do with it anything you choose. In most cases, this is done by Reframing (using it as a learning experience). Also, you may determine what you want from the situation "Control or Approval." Then go through the proper steps to release your need for Control and or Approval. You may also ask yourself what role you played in this conflict other than the victim.

To show how to Own the Problem I begin by using a metaphor. This metaphor will help the client to start thinking in a way that will help him resolve issues in his life. He will be shown how to stop blaming others and how to stop being a victim. The metaphor is as follows:

Metaphor

Let's say we have been friends for twenty years during which time I was constantly saying "I am going to Mexico to teach." Every time we speak on the phone or see one another in person I start with I am going to Mexico to teach. You, on the other hand, work and are financially struggling. You have an old nineteen seventy-two Volkswagen that is constantly breaking down and in need of repairs, which you cannot afford.

How do I know, because we are friends and you call me several times a week, at all times of the day and night, asking me to come rescue you, and of course I do. I come and tow your car home and fix the starter or generator or carburetor or whatever the problem is at that time. During this act of kindness I, of course, remind you several times that I am going to Mexico to teach.

Then one Saturday morning I call you, and when you answer the phone I say what's up, guess what, then you interrupt and say I love you but I just don't have the time to talk right now. I only have one day off and I have to get my chores done. I interrupt you with, hey, just called to say I am going to Mexico to teach, I've got my plane ticket and I'm leaving in the morning, you say really, finally, after all these years, that's great.

I called to see if you want to use my car while I'm gone. With hesitation you say I don't know, I don't think so. So, I ask, how are you going to get to work, certainly not in that Junker of a car you have. Hey, check the oil, park it in your driveway, and take care of it, then at least you can get back and forth to work. Reluctantly you agree.

Early the next morning I pick you up and off to the airport we go. When we arrive I grab my bags, give you a hug and hurry into the terminal. You roar off in my brand new

Ferrari. For the next three or four weeks you drive around, your hair blowing in the breeze, talking on the phone, visiting your friends, seeing and being seen.

Then one day you're driving on the freeway doing about a hundred and fifty miles per hour, I think that's the speed limit for a Ferrari. Then all of a sudden you hear a loud noise, the car fills with smoke, the motor quits running and you drift over to the side of the road. You get out of the car, look down the freeway and you see an oil slick starting quite a ways down the road and stopping right under the car.

With a feeling of panic, you immediately get the local Ferrari dealer on the phone. After some time the tow truck shows up and loads the car up and off to the service department you go. After you have waited for several hours, the service manager returns to inform you that you did not put oil in the car and you blew up the motor. He then states that it is going to cost one hundred thousand dollars to repair. He asks, what would you like us to do at this time?

By the way, you can't get hold of me. I'm in Walla Walla, Mexico totally enjoying myself without a care in the world. There I am on the beach: sunsets, senoritas, cervezas. There's no cell or phone service. You have to deal with it on your own.

In a state of shock, you begin to stutter, hem and haw and nearly pass out, finally you get your wits about you enough to say, just deliver it to my house and unload it in the driveway. Now, there it is this forest green monster from hell sitting right in front of you making you sick to your stomach among other things and constantly reminding you of that hundred thousand dollars that you do not have.

Every morning, the first thing you see when walking out the door is that nightmare giving you that sick feeling in the pit of your stomach. After you're at work for a few hours it slips your mind and the stress lets up a little.

However, in the afternoon as soon as you turn the corner on the street where you live, the first thing you see is that forest green monster from hell. There it is, reminding you of that hundred thousand dollars that you don't have. By the way, if you had that kind of money you certainly would not be driving a broken down seventy-two Volkswagen.

I then say to my client, *My question to you is? What are you going to do with it now?* When asked this question most people say, *I don't know, Let it sit there* or *I'd just throw a cover over it and pretend it's not there.*

At this point I pause for a while then ask, *By the way, is that how you have been handling other problems in your life? So how would you be feeling right about now knowing someday you were going to have to tell me you didn't put oil in the engine and it blew up?* Of course, their response is *Terrible.* I then ask the following questions:

Can you sell it?

Most of the time they answer *NO.* I ask why, and they respond *because it's not worth anything.* I inform them it's a Ferrari and even with a blown engine it's still worth a couple hundred thousand dollars. I then repeat the question. *Can you sell it?* They respond, *I guess, but who would buy a car with a blown engine.*

Could you make a loan against it for repairs?

They reply, *I suppose if it's really worth that much.* I reply, *Oh really, what kind of car do you have?* When they reply, I ask, *Can I make a loan against it? I could use a little extra cash.* Most of the time I get a blank stare then finally an, *I guess.*

I reply, *Let me see if I understand you. I can make a loan against your car and put the cash in "my" pocket, without you knowing?* Finally, they answer *no.* I ask, *Why?* They respond, *Because it's not yours.* I come back with a pause, *Oh!* Then let me ask you this:

Can you junk the car?

(By this time they are starting to get it.) *No, because it's not mine.* I quickly respond, *So what you are saying is, you can't sell it, you can't make a loan against it, and you can't junk it. So you're pretty much stuck with a problem that someone else owns. Is that what you're telling me?* They answer, *yes but this is confusing.*

At this point I continue with the metaphor. *So every day it's the same old thing. Every morning and every evening you're reminded of your very expensive screw up. The first thing you see when you leave in the morning and the first thing when you get home in the evening is that hundred thousand dollar nightmare. This continues for about two months.*

Then one day you receive a phone call from me. When you answer the phone I say, hey how's everything going with you? As you begin to talk I interrupt and say, what's wrong. Your voice sounds a little stressed and flat. For some reason you just don't sound like your cheery self.

You reply very softly, *I blew the engine up in your car.* I say *What!* You reply, *I'm so sorry I didn't put oil in your car and I blew the engine up. I have no idea how to repay you or how to get it fixed. It will cost a hundred thousand dollars for repairs.*

I answer back, *don't worry about it, if that's the worst thing that happens to us, we have it made. I called to tell you that I'm not coming back. I want you to put my house on the market, send me a few things, keep what you want and sell or donate the rest.*

Oh by the way, since I don't need the car here in paradise with the sunsets, senoritas and cervezas, I'll send you the title as soon as I have a chance. So relax and don't let things get to you so easily. This is not going to stop the world from turning.

In a few weeks or so you receive a letter from me and enclosed is the title to the car signed over to you free and clear. I now ask the client, *Now that you have the title what are you going to do with the car/problem?* Most of the time the reply is *Sell it.*

I then ask, *what is the difference now, than earlier in the story?* Usually their response is *Well, now it's mine.* I follow up with, *so what is the moral of the story?* Nine out of ten times I get *I don't know. Don't borrow anyone's car, always check the oil, I don't know, what is it?*

I then respond, the moral of the story is, *You can't do anything with anything unless you own it. When you have a problem and you blame it on other people, places, things or events, "they own it." And you can't do anything but be stuck with it.*

You must find a way to take ownership of your part if you are involved in any form. Then and only then can you resolve your part of the issue and rid yourself of the emotional pain. Once you own the problem the necessary course of action can be taken to neutralize the pain.

It becomes very easy to make excuses for ourselves as well as others, so we don't have to make a few hard decisions. To be happy, you must first find what is between you and your happiness. This may require you to change your beliefs in some areas. It may also require therapy, education, working on your self-esteem, reframing past events, or various other things.

After the client has discovered the issues he must own whatever he is upset about and/or involved in, then the Life Coach can then lead him through the process of releasing the Want of Control or the Want of Approval. Going through this exercise and actually releasing the other party or parties involved will resolve his role in the issue. This will not solve the other people's problem; that is up to them.
(Refer to Control/Approval and Voice)

Life Cycles

Over the years, I have paid close attention to the age of people who have come to see me. I found many of them have similarities at certain ages in their lives. This insight may help the Life Coach attain a more comprehensive perception of the client. Explaining these Life Cycles to the client may help ease the emotional pain.

This is the case, especially if he is going through a particularly rough time in his life. Explaining these cycles can help him to understand what he is experiencing may be normal for that particular age. It is merely a time for change and growth, even though this change and growth may be unwanted and may seem disastrous.

Knowing the age of a person will help you to understand the era they grew up in and give you some insight into their norms and possibly their expectations. What was socially acceptable fifty years ago, in the workplace, is no longer acceptable today. Management techniques have changed dramatically.

This is evident as companies send their managers to sensitivity training, sexual harassment classes, and many other training seminars on how to treat people and basically adapt to the ever-changing environment. As society changes it puts pressure on those people of an earlier era to make changes that may not seem natural to them.

Smoking is another example of how people are forced to change and the stresses they experience which are displayed in their behaviors and health issues. What was once sexy and macho and the norm is now viewed as an unhealthy, dirty habit. Thousands of dollars are spent annually by people trying to break the habit.

There always seems to be something that happens which will cause us to move from one cycle to the next. Marital problems, an illness or death of a loved one, loss of employment, or even our own health issues can trigger the changes. How well a person is equipped to deal with changes will directly affect the way he manages and deals with these changing life cycles.

These are the cycles we experience throughout our life. Some of these cycles seem to be biological, while others seem to be sociological. Even some of what appears to be biological may be triggered by some sociological event. For example, being under constant stress can affect our health, thus triggering biological conditions.

Some biological cycles seems to trigger certain sociological changes in all of us as individuals. An example of this would be puberty, at age thirteen for most. Here, a biological cycle begins and brings with it changes, not only in bodily functions and interest in the opposite sex, but also changes in social behavior.

Shortly after puberty, a more rebellious attitude toward parents and authority quickly develops. Generally, at about age fourteen to fifteen, it's as though one night the parents went out to dinner across town and ate dumb food. Then around ages twenty-two to twenty-three, they go to the other side of town and eat smart food. We wonder how they got so smart so quickly.

Life Cycles

Birth to puberty	Innocent, developing personality
13 – 20	Rebellious, parents become dumb
21 – 22	Parents become smart, ask their advice
26 – 27	Come into knowing, we know we know
32	Begin to wonder about things / our beliefs
33	Begin to doubt things and our beliefs
34	Question our beliefs / life, religion, etc.
35 - 39	Everything seems to come unraveled
	Relationship breakups soar
	Questions like, what is life all about
	Halfway through life, not successful
	Men start doing things they did in their twenties looking for knowing
39 – 42	Begin to find answers, put life back together with new concepts, new priorities
47	If cycle avoided, comes again with less intensity
52 - 57	Cycle starts again, much less intensity
	Takes a significant happening to bring change

There are those who continue on the same path, only they become hardened and have resentment toward the opposite sex, the government, etc. In short, they generally become very negative. This is not a scientific research, but my observations from working with all age groups for more than thirty years.

Between the ages of twenty-one to twenty-three we tend to realize our parents are not so dumb after all. We may even seek out their advice on things. Of course, it is not the parents, but us going through our own particular cycle. Our parents have their own issues.

Around the age of twenty-seven there is a very subtle change. This change may not come to our awareness until one day we realize this is what it's like to be an adult. It seems to give us a sense of knowing. In fact, we know we know and, if asked, we let you know that we know.

This sense of knowing continues until about the age of thirty-two. Think back to that time in your life. You may have been in the military, you may have been married with children, or may have just been trying to make a living when that thought came into your awareness.

At the age of thirty-two something begins to happen. We are not prepared for the beginning of what will be a ten-year-cycle. At this age, we frequently begin to wonder about more profound things in life such as what is life all about, what is our role.

These thoughts and wonderings begin to build in intensity as we enter our thirty-third year. At this age we begin to doubt our beliefs, our decisions, our wants, needs and desires. By this time, all of that knowing that we know has dissipated into confusion and doubt.

Age thirty-four brings on the questions. We question our purpose, if we thought we had any inkling of one. We question our beliefs, life, religion, and just about everything else. This year is the precursor to the next year, which is the unraveling.

At age thirty-five it all seems to come unraveled. All of that knowing, all of that confidence, all of what we had come to believe is unraveling. It seems nothing can be done. Relationship breakups soar even though we try to find common ground. Both individual's needs and views seem to change and they become at odds with one another.

Questions like, "What is life all about?" may keep coming to mind. "I'm not happy and can't seem to pinpoint why." "I'm half way through my life and still not successful." "If only he or she would do something different I might be able to get a handle on what is happening to me." "It seems like the world has turned against me."

Over the years I have heard people express their anguish in many different phrases and terms. I will say to them, "Sitting here talking with you I can tell you are a smart, intelligent person. My question to you is, Why do you think nature put you in this situation? Why do you think you are going through this pain?" Of course, their answer is: "I don't have a clue, and I don't like it one bit."

I then ask, "Who are you when you are not a dad (mom) or a husband (wife)? Who are you when you are not an employee or a boss? Who are you when you are not a son (daughter)? Who are you when you are not a good friend? Who are you as an individual and what is your Purpose?"

"Do you think maybe nature has you in this situation for that reason so you can discover a deeper you? Would you consider that possibly it's time to reconsider some of your priorities? Perhaps it's time to review some ego-driven behaviors and attitudes. Maybe it's time to take a look at yourself and your life from a different angle."

Success can have different meanings to different people. To some, it can mean money, yet to others it can be a happy, loving relationship. Others may view success as something spiritual. Each person can have their own twist to the meaning of success.

The Life Coach will need to listen for the client to reveal his own vision of success. It is important to refocus on the positives and begin reframing the negatives or the things that are perceived as wrong. It's very easy to lose sight of what is important in an individual's life with all of the day-to-day stress.

It has been my experience working with men going through this stage in their life that they begin to go in search of knowing. Some call this their "mid-life crisis." They will have a tendency to date younger women. These younger women see them as stable and successful, when in reality, they are going through the roughest time in their life.

They begin doing things they did in their twenties. They are searching for "knowing." In their late twenties and early thirties they were confident and had a sense of knowing. Somewhere along the way they lost "it" and can't seem to get "it" back.

When all else fails and they can't find what they are looking for in the past, the fortunate ones begin reading self-help books and going to counseling for help. Here the internal journey begins. Between the ages of thirty-nine and forty-two they begin to find answers and incorporate them into their life. These answers include new concepts and new priorities which help them put their life back together.

For others, that feeling of being lost continues as they avoid the internal journey by continuing to look outside of themselves for answers. However, that urge to find what is missing in life comes again at about the age of forty-seven. The intensity of this feeling/urge is much less than earlier.

For those who continue to refuse to go inside in search of balance, that urge returns at about fifty-two. Again, the intensity to do something about it is much less at this age than in the past. These individuals seem to become hardened and what some may think as being negatively opinionated.

It's been my experience that it "usually" takes a significant happening in their life to bring about a change in attitude and beliefs. If changes are not made at about this age, these people tend to not make what I call spiritual changes. This does not necessarily mean something will not happen in their life to trigger change.

I have actually had individuals in their seventies and eighties come to me for a particular issue and end up working on issues that have kept them stuck in a belief that has not worked in their best interest for many years. Each person is unique, even though we share many similarities at certain ages and stages of life.

It is important to note that a significant happening can cause an individual to move forward in the cycle process or move back to a simpler time, even to a point when someone has to care for them. The death of a child, spouse, sibling, or parent may be more than some individuals are equipped to handle.

For some, it may cause them to mature much faster than they would otherwise. They seem to take life by the horns and grow up fast. For others, it is devastating and the trauma seems to, paralyze them emotionally. They simply give up and go into a "just existing" mode.

(Refer to Perceptual Defense Mechanism, Regression)

The Life Coach can use the Life Cycle tool to gain insight into the client's way of thinking and possibly their situation. The reason they believe and do the things they do, in many cases, can be traced back to an era of their formative years.

Asset List

The Asset List is not a list of your belongings, your investments, or other physical assets that you may possess or hold. It is a list of attributes, characteristics and behaviors that you may or may not "live your life by." It is a way for an individual to make the changes he wants in his life

Making your Asset List is a way of programming or reprogramming yourself to have a more positive disposition or outlook about yourself and others. It can be used to make a variety of changes. You can use it to fulfill a dream, get an education, lose weight; it can even be used in the process of breaking addictions. It can be adapted and used in conjunction with many of the tools described in this manual.

Many of these characteristics and behaviors may have been developed early in life when you were trying to get your wants, needs and desires met. These behaviors can include, but are not limited to, being an Intimidator, an Interrogator, an Aloof Person, or a Poor Me (Victim). Each of these behavior types has their own struggles. These behavioral issues cause problems for people in the way they treat others and the effect it has on them and their self-worth.

The Intimidator actually bullies others to gain his power. Even though he may not realize it, he shows disrespect for himself and others. I have found the Intimidator thinks there is nothing wrong with his aggressive behavior. However, he can quickly shift to being the Victim when someone with a strong personality stands up to him.

The Interrogator's "need to know" prompts him to ask questions to the point of having others feeling as though they are being interrogated. The more others attempt to avoid being interrogated, the more he questions. This type does not connect their questioning with others attempt to avoid them.

The Aloof gains his power from being quiet. Others feel they have done something wrong because the Aloof doesn't share what he is thinking. With all of their questions, the Interrogator can cause someone to become Aloof. Because of their silence, the Aloof can cause those close to him to become Interrogators.

The Poor Me (Victim) gains his power from playing the victim role. They are always complaining of their bad breaks, health issues, or woes that have befallen them. This can cause others to avoid them because of their constant complaints. Any one of these dramas can cause many problems in relationships, both personal and professional. *(Refer to Control Dramas)*

The Asset List can be used to rectify Control Dramas and many of the problems they cause. It is a great tool to use when building self-esteem and confidence. It works well when working with relationship problems. The tool is especially good when the client is dealing with a breakup and wants to make changes so he can reconcile with his partner, providing the partner is willing.

After listening to the client tell his version of what has taken place, the Life Coach will want to ask a series of questions; however, he will need to listen carefully for attributes that may be missing in the client's behavior and thought process.

As he reveals things about himself that he may be unaware of, the Life Coach will be flagging certain things. For example, is he understanding, forgiving, compassionate, kind, and gentle? Is he rigid, opinionated, and non-yielding to others? Does he have a disrespecting attitude in general?

Basically, the Life Coach is listening for the client's role in the breakup or the problems he is having. The Life Coach will then design questions around those characteristics. As the client answers the questions, the Life Coach will put the answers on the whiteboard. *(Use only the positive aspect of the answer and keep it to one or two words)*

Often I am asked during the first session with new clients what they can do to begin to make changes. My response is to tell them to begin by making an asset list. You begin this list by taking a large piece of poster board and draw a line down the center. On the left side at the top you label it

"Who I Am." On the right side at the top you label it "Who I Am Becoming."

As a constant reminder, I put my Asset List on the bedroom wall. It was the first thing I saw in the morning when I awoke and the last thing I saw before going to sleep. Every time you walk past your Asset List, whether you are consciously aware of it or not, your subconscious mind is reminded of who you are and who you are becoming according to the list.

On the Asset List you write the behaviors or characteristics only in the positive form. For example, if you are unhappy, write on the "Who I Am Becoming" side, "more and more happy." If you truly believe in your heart of hearts that you are compassionate then write the word "compassionate," on the "Who I Am" side of your Asset List.

If not, write the word "compassionate" on the "Who I Am Becoming" side. There can be no sometimes, or now and then; you either are, all of the time, or you are not. If the answer is sometimes, or now and then, the word compassionate must be written on the "Who I Am Becoming" side.

Asset List

Who I Am	Who I Am Becoming
intelligent	more understanding
trustworthy	forgiving
good-looking	compassionate
sexy	kind
hard-working	gentle
secure	more and more flexible
financially secure	caring of others opinions
	willing to listen to others
	respectful of others
	loyal
	loving
	educated

The **Asset List** is an excellent way to reprogram or program oneself to make positive changes. Coupled with a daily meditation routine in front of the **Asset List** will enhance the process of acquiring desired outcomes.

To begin the Asset List, The Life Coach will use the behaviors and characteristics that the client wants to change or reinforce. To help the client begin coming up with things on their own the Life Coach can give the client a few of the following suggestions:

Are you intelligent, trustworthy, pretty, loyal, loving, sexy, hard-working, secure, educated, and/or financially secure? Put the ones you already are on the "Who I Am" side. If not, put it on the "Who I am Becoming" side. There is no sometimes, I think I am, or I try to be. You either are or you are not.

As you think of things throughout the day that you are or want to change, jot them down so you don't forget to put them on your Asset List when you get home. Be sure to write each one large enough so that you can see the words from across the room. Adding to your list is a continual process, even as you begin to change.

Put your Asset List in a place where it's easily seen from where you can comfortably sit and read your affirmations. I have had several clients tell me they turned one of the rooms in their home into a meditation room. They installed special lighting, surround sound, and other amenities, which are all right but that might be a little overkill for meditation.

You do not need to set aside a special room; however, I do suggest when you meditate you make it special. Light a candle, have a special mat or throw rug, create a special ambience; make this time a special event. It can take place in your bedroom, living room, or wherever you choose. Just make it a special event.

After you have begun the physical aspect of your Asset List by writing down the characteristics and behaviors you want to change or reinforce, it is now time for the mental step. This next step involves meditation: clearing the mind, getting rid of the chatter, and inviting the changes to take place.

Set aside time each day, at least once each day, or preferably two times (1/2 hour to 45 minutes, minimum). This step then requires meditation. When I suggest this step to nearly all of my clients, their responses are pretty much the same: "I don't know how to meditate, I can't sit still that long, my mind wanders from one thing to the next, I don't know how to clear my mind, I don't have the time."

My response to them is, "If out of twenty four hours you can't take thirty minutes to an hour for yourself, then I think it's obvious why you have the problems that you have." Then I explain, "If you are going to start an arts and crafts project or cook a nice dinner, you first must clear off the workspace."

It works the same for making changes in your life. You must first clear your mind so you can begin the process of self-discovery. I personally believe it's the most important project you will ever encounter. To embark upon a journey into self to get to know the real you of you can be the most rewarding venture in your life.

The process that I use, and the one I suggest the Life Coach use with clients, is as follows: Put on some soft, non-rhythmic, meditation type music. Sit quietly and comfortably in front of your Asset List and with your eyes open, stare at the list. If your eyes find a specific word, it's okay to stare at that particular word.

At this point refer to the meditation mentioned earlier. Simply make a few adjustments at the beginning and adapt it to the Asset List rather than Purpose or Plan. The client is actually reprogramming himself by being the one choosing the negative thoughts and behaviors he wants to change.

(Refer to Meditation)

To assist the client with his changes, the Life Coach can develop a hypnosis script using the words the client has on his Asset List. For continuity, I will use some of the aforementioned behaviors and characteristics. These questions are to help the Life Coach help his client begin to dig deeper into himself.

Below are a few of the sample questions I ask my clients and the client's "example" answers in parenthesis. Note the questions the Life Coach will ask will be based on information gathered during the pre-talk. The Life Coach will pose any suggestions in the form of questions.

In the following paragraph my questions are in regular font and the clients "answers" are parenthesis and italics.

Are you understanding *(sometimes)*, forgiving *(no)*, compassionate *(not really)*, kind *(sometimes)*, and gentle *(no)*. Put the foregoing on the "Who I'm Becoming" side of the Asset List. Are you rigid *(probably)* Replace with, *more and more flexible*. Opinionated *(yes)* Replace with *caring of others' opinions*. Non-yielding *(yes)* Replace with *willing to listen to others*.

Do you have a disrespecting attitude in general *(I've been told that)* Replace with *respectful of others*. Are you intelligent *(yes)*, trustworthy *(absolutely)*, good-looking *(yes)*, loyal *(can be)*, loving *(sometimes)*, sexy *(yes)*, hard-working *(yes)*, secure *(yes)*, educated *(somewhat)*, financially secure *(yes)*. You can see where this goes.

The Life Coach will first do an induction and then blend the client's choices into the script. The induction can be a simple relaxation. Have the client close his eyes, take a few deep breaths, and have him go through his body relaxing all of his muscles and organs.

The following is an example of a hypnosis script using the answers from a client. Notice the repetition and the different ways it is put into context. Keep in mind, repetition is very important in hypnosis.

Hypnosis Script

As you sit there relaxing..... your thoughts drifting..... your mind wandering..... and you moving deeper and deeper into a deep level of self-actualization..... I am going to speak to your subconscious mind..... which will begin assisting you..... in making the changes..... that you have been outlining.

So just continue to let your conscious thoughts..... and mind..... drift and wander..... about whatever you choose..... Because I will be speaking to that part of you..... that is in charge of making the changes..... in the way you think..... in the way you feel..... in the way you behave.

Your mind, body and spirit..... will be working together..... with your wants, needs and desires..... to bring these changes..... to your conscious, your subconscious and your unconscious mind..... the changes you need to make..... to bring peace, harmony and tranquility..... into your everyday life.

In fact..... it really is in your best interest..... for you to start right now..... becoming more understanding...... It's good for you..... your family..... and those you love..... for you to be more and more understanding and forgiving. Just imagine..... how great it will be to have others respect you..... because of how compassionate, kind and understanding you have become.

Just think what it is going to be like..... for you to become open..... to new ways of doings things..... and by you being more approachable..... you become more respected in every way. Respect is a quality of self-esteem..... and of course you are developing more and more self-esteem..... as I speak to you.

You know..... you know deep within you..... deep down past all of the fears..... down past the old programming..... deep down past those childish behaviors..... that you have been using to protect yourself. You no longer need that false childish front you've been using..... because now you are an adult.

And you know as an adult..... it requires you to use different behaviors..... then when you were young..... Yes it is true you are intelligent..... trustworthy..... hard-working..... and financially secure. However..... it is now time for you to make changes..... in other areas..... of who you are as an adult.

Even with all of those fine attributes..... it's time to realize there are changes which need to be made..... on all levels..... Changes in the way you think..... changes in the way you feel..... and changes in the way you behave..... These changes are good..... these changes are good for you..... on all levels..... of who you are...... and who you are becoming. These changes are good..... because they are from you, to you, for you, of you, by you, because of you..... of course they are good..... of course they are good.

Here..... Now..... You..... in this deep state of self-actualization..... you find yourself being more flexible..... more gentle with others and yourself..... in every way..... You..... now realize..... down there where all of these changes are taking place..... that it is time for you to listen to the opinions of others.

This simply means..... you are being respectful of others and yourself as well..... Listening to others..... caring about their opinion..... and being respectful..... simply means you have given up those childish ways..... for the ways of an adult..... which of course you are..... Now..... realize it's time to make these mature changes.

In this process of changing the way you think..... the way you feel..... and the way you behave..... you find other positives qualities emerging within you..... You find yourself being more loving..... more tender..... more loyal..... in the way you think and the way you behave.

As these changes continue..... you will find yourself having the desire..... to learn more about yourself..... and educate yourself..... in whatever interests you. Take this time to welcome all of these positive changes..... which will bring happiness, peace, harmony in all aspects of your life.

Here..... now..... you in this deep state of self-actualization..... you now..... experience..... all of the changes of which you are becoming..... You now..... welcome the fact..... that you are more understanding than you have ever been..... and you are becoming more understanding with each passing day.

These changes naturally lead you to be..... more caring of others opinions..... more flexible..... more forgiving..... compassionate..... kind, gentle and loving of yourself and others..... and this is good..... These changes let you experience these good feelings..... all the way..... to the very core of your being.

You now begin to experience..... a sense of peace..... and balance in your life..... as the desire to be loyal to yourself and others'..... It becomes obvious..... that it is in your best interest..... on many levels of your identity. In your best interest to make these changes..... in the way you think..... in the way you feel..... and the way you behave..... toward yourself and others.

Oh it is true..... that it's good for your self-esteem and confidence..... to know and believe..... that you are intelligent..... trustworthy..... good-looking..... sexy..... hard-working..... secure within yourself..... and financially secure as well.

All of these changes taking place within you..... will only change your life for the better..... Now let yourself feel how good it feels..... to feel good..... about feeling good..... about feeling good about yourself. You now welcome the positive changes..... into your life with open arms..... and an open heart.

I am going to count from one to five..... when I say five and only when I say five..... will you open your eyes..... feeling good in every way.

Here the Life Coach will count from one to five bringing the client out of the hypnotic state. During the count-out, make sure to interject several post-hypnotic suggestions between each number. It is important to count slowly so the client has time to finish processing all of the suggestions given during the session.

I normally count from one to four using several relevant post-hypnotic suggestions. I then start over at number one and count to five having the client let his eyes become moist and his breathing pick up and the sounds of my voice calls him up. Then on the number five I snap my fingers and say, "Just open your eyes feeling good in every way."

Notice I never directly mentioned the Control Dramas in the script. I covered the Intimidator, Interrogator, Aloof and the Poor Me by making suggestions about respect of self and others, changing childish behaviors and becoming an adult. The following paragraph is an excerpt from the script showing how they were covered:

You know..... you know deep within you..... deep down past all of the fears..... down past the old programming..... deep down past those childish behaviors..... that you have been using to protect yourself. You no longer need that false childish front you've been using..... because you are an adult now. And you know as an adult..... it requires you to use different behaviors..... than when you were young.

Voice

The purpose of working with the Voice is to get the client's emotions involved. The Voice plays a crucial role when making changes having to do with matters of the heart. This is especially true when working on releasing the Want of Control and the Want of Approval.

Most of us have heard and can tell the difference between the sound and resonation in the voice of "The Valley Girl" persona. It comes from high in the throat and/or up into the facial mask sounding somewhat nasally. It sounds and resonates much differently than someone who is sincere and speaks with conviction in their voice.

When speaking, we should be able to feel our Voice resonate through every muscle and every cell in our body. Try closing your eyes and placing the center of your palm over your heart chakra. This is located just about where your cleavage would start. Make sure the very center of the palm of your hand is over the heart chakra.

Take a few seconds and focus your attention on your chest and hand. Now slowly say your complete address aloud and see if you can feel your voice resonate through your chest and out through the palm of your hand. If not, begin moving your hand slightly up or down until you experience the location of the strongest vibration.

The Life Coach may find as I did that the majority will find their hand will be moved upward to the throat. The purpose here is to help the individual recognize from where his voice is resonating. The objective then will be to move his voice into the heart region so the release can take place on an emotional level.

Many times an individual will find it very difficult to get his voice to resonate from the center of his chest and out through the palm of his hand. If there is no success after several attempts, I will place my hand on my chest and have him place his hand on mine.

<u>Voice</u>

The stance demonstrates the placement of the hands to determine **Voice** resonation. The left hand is to be placed on the center of the back between the shoulder blades. The right hand is placed over the heart charka. Here is from where the **Voice** must resonate.

I begin talking, explaining the process of the exercise or saying my address so they can feel my voice resonate not only through my hand but through theirs as well. I then go back to them and proceed through the process. I help them to begin the process of getting their voice resonating through their chest and hand now that they know what to expect.

If they still have difficulty, I will use the following technique: As soon as their Voice begins to resonate through their heart chakra I immediately go back into the release process. During this session or in a previous session, I gather information about their life, their loved ones, and anyone else who may be near and dear to them. Experience has taught me to be prepared just in case I need the information, which I do nine out of ten times.

The technique goes along these lines: I place the center of their right-hand palm on their chest directly over their heart chakra. I then place my hand on theirs. At the same time I put my left hand on their back opposite my right hand. I very softly speak to them. I ask them to imagine their child (or loved one) is in the hospital and it's a life or death situation. I tell them the doctor informs you there is nothing more he can do; it's now up to your child and God.

I then have them imagine being in the hospital room alone with their child. I explain to them that they only have one chance to sincerely, from their heart, ask God to please save their child. I ask them to visualize or imagine their Voice coming from deep within their heart, through their chest, and out through their hand.

Very softly I ask them to repeat after me, *"Oh God please don't let my baby die (loved one, name them) please don't take my baby from me."* In most cases, this stirs their emotions enough to temporarily move their voice so it resonates through their heart chakra. With a little coaching, it lasts long enough to complete the exercise so the release can take place.

As soon as they get their Voice resonating from their heart chakra, I immediately have them use the same tone and pitch and sincerity in their voice as they go through releasing the Want of Control or the releasing the Want of Approval. It helps if the Life Coach uses the tone and pitch in his voice which he is attempting to evoke in the client.

I will continue to work with those individuals that are at first unable to get their Voice to resonate from the center of their chest. I use whatever information I had previously gathered during the pre-talk that might help facilitate the process. This must be an emotional release.

We go through the process until they can feel the feeling of desperation in their body, mainly in their chest. I remind them the release must come from the heart not the head, for the heart is where the emotional pain is held. It's from the heart that it must be released.

Much of where the Voice resonates from has to do with the subconscious perception of past programming and its effect on a person's self-esteem and self-confidence. Keep in mind the subconscious mind is a "yes" mind; it takes everything as truth whether direct or inferred. This is true especially when we are children.

The movement of the Voice away from the heart charka is the subconscious's attempt to protect our feelings or our heart from emotional pain. These past experiences can hamper the Voice from initially resonating from the heart charka. We've all heard the phrases, "that's a head person," or "that's a heart person," "he's a thinker" or "he wears his feelings on his sleeve."

It is to the advantage of the Life Coach to understand the movement of the Voice and its connection to the emotions. The resonation of the Voice and where it is resonating from is vital when using the Voice as a tool in the process of releasing the Want of Control and the Want of Approval.

It is also true when working with forgiveness. Saying you forgive and feeling it at the core of your being, can be two different things. True forgiveness is an experience, not something that is said because it's a nice thing to say. Forgiveness involves reframing the effect a particular experience had on the emotions.

From the heart chakra the Voice moves in four directions. It moves down into the abdomen into the solar plexus region or up into the throat and even into the head. It also can resonate in the back and even behind you. It may also resonate in the front or out in front of you.

It has been my experience from doing this exercise over the years, when the voice comes from deep within the abdomen or the region of the solar plexus, the voice will be deep or gruff and/or harsh. I have found that this has to do with a "pushing away" effect. By pushing away, I mean this type of individual pushes people away in fear that others may find out that he doesn't know much or, for that part, anything, so he keeps others at a distant with his deep gruff Voice.

When the resonation of the individual's voice has moved from the heart chakra area up into the throat or head, this person is guarding his heart. He is guarding his heart/feelings with his logic and does not add depth or feelings to what is being communicated. This does not mean they do not feel emotional pain. In fact, they can be quite emotional.

This gradual shift in the Voice is a subconscious maneuver and is below the person's level of awareness. The reasons for this maneuver can range from some past significant negative experience to just a need to fit in with the "in crowd." Whatever the reason, it goes unnoticed because it seems natural. The Voice will be a higher pitch than that of the one resonating from the heart charka or the one that comes from deep in the abdomen.

When the Voice resonates from the individual's back, you may find this person is shy and withdrawn. They project a demeanor of not being worthy or good enough. As this person talks, it seems their mouth moves and then the words seem to follow a nanosecond or so later.

It is as though their true esoteric self is standing behind them. When they speak, there is a time lapse from when their mouth physically moves and the words actually come through their lips. Usually these individuals are soft-spoken. To assist them in releasing the Want of Control or the Want of Approval, it is imperative that they move the resonation of their voice forward into the heart chakra area.

When the Voice is projected out in front of the individual, he is attempting to project something that he himself does not believe to be true about himself. This misdirection is a projection of what he wants others to think about him and what he stands for or how he may feel about himself.

He will appear to have a more grandiose type of complex, which is a self-esteem issue, even though he may appear to have self-esteem and self-confidence. This type of projection demonstrates that he is over-compensating for something he is either hiding from or lacking in his life.

These individuals seem to take a stand and refuse to consider certain other facts because they are afraid of being wrong. I have also found that the roots of this disconnect is often based in the early years of their life. It seems his need to be right is more important than actually being correct. In this type of person, the voice will be high in the upper chest or throat and seems to come from out in front of them.

Helping someone to center their thoughts, feelings, and emotions through their Voice can play a major role in their journey to self-discovery. The Life Coach will want to keep in mind when working with an individual who is trying to release control or approval that the objective is to first get the voice to resonate from the center of the chest.

This may require several attempts. I have learned the Voice found its place of resonation in the individual when he was young and moving it is not always an easy task. However, it is a necessary task. The Life Coach may have to get a little creative in an attempt to tap into the client's emotions.

The release must come from their heart and not from their head. In most cases, their head and their heart are at odds with one another on certain issues. When attempting a release on matters of the heart using the head, the release does not work. So it is essential to get the voice centered with the heart chakra, even if it isn't as strong as you may like.

I have a few techniques I use to assist the person in moving their voice to the area of the heart chakra. First, I explain to them the process of identifying and owning the issue. If necessary, I will use the aforementioned technique about the hospital scene.

We then go through the process of releasing using the information gathered. While they are learning the process using their head, I begin working with centering their voice so, when we actually go through the exercise, the release will take place.

When the release takes place, it will be followed by a deep sigh or a light feeling like a weight has been lifted. At this point, the Life Coach may want to wait a few moments and then ask the client how he feels. You may also wait awhile and watch for the client to take a sigh.
(Refer to Control/Approval)

When working with any of the tools in this manual or any of the client's behaviors, the Life Coach will want to pay close attention to the resonation of the Voice. It will help to determine the disconnect between who the client projects to be and his real sense of self. Keep in mind, the client will be unaware of the imbalance of his Voice and the emotional disconnect.

The following example is an attempt to explain how the emotional disconnect can take place without a person being aware of what is taking place. It resembles the development of how an attitude is formed within an individual. This happens much the same as how a corporate culture within a business is developed over the years. It happens slowly and consistently and becomes very difficult to change.

Imagine owning a business with all of the different departments involved in running it efficiently. Let's say it is a construction company. You will need a sales department, estimating department, and an accounting department which will include accounts payable, accounts receivable.

You may need a design department, as well as a department that handles employees and subcontractors. You may possibly require a department to deal with vendors and purchasing, just to mention a few. Needless to say, there is going to be a lot of paperwork generated.

Each of these departments will need their own filing cabinets and systems to keep their records organized. Depending on the size of the contract, each job may take up an entire drawer, or more, in a particular file cabinet. Because of its size, a certain contract may have a dedicated cabinet of its own.

After the contract is complete and all of the paperwork is done, as the job is being closed, you have someone write a summary, including all departments, the key points, and highlights of the contract. Here you would briefly list all major problems and their solutions.

This can be used for a quick reference if it should be needed in the future because of a problem or a similar job. This file would be placed in the front of all the files for that particular job. All the other files will support that summary in detail and what has taken place with that contract. It also serves as part of a "buried memory" of what has happened within your company.

As the years go by, you slowly develop a corporate culture based on those "buried memories." You may not remember all of the details of every contract; however, you will remember highlights from those summaries. Even though you may have forgotten the details from the many things which happened over the years, they still play an important role in how you do business and the decisions you make.

The same goes for the individual who has buried memories of things that happened throughout his life. He dealt with them the best he could at the time and moved on with life. Some things taught him a lesson, while others got repressed into his subconscious because he wasn't equipped to handle them at the time.

After some years go by, the individual is left with beliefs, behaviors, and attitudes which may not be working in his best interest. His "corporate culture" attitude will require some serious changes; however, it will not be an easy task sorting through the archives of his memories.

All of his experiences can have a direct effect on the Voice. The Life Coach, being aware of the Voice and its location and resonation, gives him insight into locating a good starting point to begin the process of making deep and lasting positive life changes.

Ten-Year Plan

The Ten-Year Plan is a road map to achieving wants and desires. When I ask new clients to do a ten-year plan they laugh and say they don't know what they are going to be doing next week much less than ten years from now. Very quickly they let me know they don't have that much self-discipline.

They tell me how chaotic and out of control their life has become. They also say they have no idea where to start a plan. They do let me know of their depression and many other issues they deal with on a daily basis. With frustration in their voice, they will sigh and say how it seems their life is going nowhere.

I tell them their life is going nowhere because they have given it to other people. I remind them that if they don't take charge of their life, someone else will take charge of it for them, and that is exactly what is happening. At some point, they must make some changes if they are going to take it back. Their typical response is, "How or where do I start, and what do I have to change?"

My response is, "You start with making a Ten-Year Plan and you start Now. You first decide what you would like to do and some of the things you would like to accomplish within the next ten years. Forget about all of the reasons why it won't work and begin thinking of the reasons it will work."

"You do not have to write them in blood or chisel them into stone, at least not at this time. Let's just explore some avenues that may help you take charge of your life. Who knows, you may find Purpose along the way, and you may be surprised what positive changes take place in your life."

"You do not need to turn your world upside down all at once. You begin by making a plan and implementing different aspects as it evolves. Keep in mind, you don't get a second chance at life so we have to get it right the first time through."

I tell my clients something I had heard when I was very young: "If you would have started ten years ago you would be there now." So in my twenties I said to myself, "If I want to 'be there' in ten years, I had better get started now." At the time I wasn't sure where "there" was, how to get there or what it consisted of but I knew I had to start somewhere.

I did know I had hopes and dreams as a child through my adolescence of what I wanted to do when I grew up. It's true, that some were not realistic; they were immature childhood fantasies. However, for the most part, they were realistic. So, that was my trigger and I started making a Ten-Year Plan. I then began diligently working on my plan to fulfill my wants and desires. I have always had a Ten-Year Plan even to this very day.

One of the reasons for a Ten-Year Plan is to take care of those unforeseen problems that seem to come out of nowhere. Having a Ten-Year Plan gives time to take the detours needed to handle those issues and get back on track. My experience from working with others, that is a two-or three-year plan can lead to problems.

The problems can result from something happening and as recovery is being dealt with, the plan gets replaced with the problem. The timetable runs out and leaves feelings of loss of control, failure, depression, and a host of other issues. Two or three years can go by very quickly when working on real issues.

Things like paying off credit cards, paying off a mortgage, and working to get out of debt can take several years. Going back to school to get or finish a degree may take three or four years or more depending on how much time is needed to put into this effort. Many unforeseen things can happen and this is one of the reasons for a Ten-Year Plan and not a two- or three-year plan.

Don't be afraid to dream a little, but it is important to be realistic. For example, if you are a hundred thousand dollars in debt and only earn ten dollars an hour, it is unrealistic to think you are going to pay off everything and save a million dollars in a few years. Of course, it is a game changer should you have a nice inheritance coming very soon.

It is realistic to make a plan to go back to school, get a better paying job, and pay off the debt. With so many online degree programs, it is feasible to accomplish just about anything you have in mind.

Once that is taken care of, then you can write into your plan how you are going to save and do the other things you want to accomplish. I always tell my clients, to achieve your goals remember first you have to *"want to," not like to*, or *wish to*. You have to *want to*, really *want to*, more than anything.

You may have to do several rough drafts before your plan begins to become a realistic road map to your desires. For example, you plan to finish a degree in the fourth year but you find you do not have the funds or enough time to dedicate solely to school, so you must move your completion date to the sixth year, thus affecting other aspects of the plan, hence causing other adjustments.

Along the way, things may change giving the opportunity to move much faster or perhaps things may cause you to make other adjustments. Basically, we are allowing for unforeseen events which may have a negative effect on the Ten-Year Plan.

Caring for children or other family members may change your circumstances and lend to rethinking some aspects of your plan. Whatever the changes, you simply plan around them and continue on, even if you have to push some things out another five years. This keeps you and your purpose alive even if at times it is a struggle.

When working with couples who are having relationship problems, many times I will use the Ten-Year Plan tool. I will have them remember back to when they were planning and working together. I ask them to remember how well they got along when they shared a common purpose.

I have each of them make a rough draft of their own Ten-Year Plan without any input from one another. I instruct them not to share what they are putting on their individual plan. Of course, I get some pretty strange looks and comments like, "I thought we were supposed to be doing this together."

There is a reason for them doing separate plans and not discussing their plan with one another. If they do one shared plan together, whichever one of them is dominant will over run the other and the plan becomes the dominant one's plan. The other simply goes along to save an argument. Needless to say, this kind of plan will not endure the test of time.

Once the personal plans are made, they bring their individual plans to their next session. Their individual plan can involve each other but just can't be shared while in the developmental stage. During their session, I explain the rules for combining the two plans into one workable Ten-Year Plan.

Our objective is to combine both plans so neither one of the individuals feels slighted. I explain to them that before either of them can give up something they have on their plan, they must convince me with a legitimate reason. It has to be a better reason than "it doesn't really matter" or "if it bothers him (her) it's not important." It is important or it would not be on their plan. This third-party intervention (the Life Coach) assures a combined agreeable compromise as the plan is developed.

So, let's begin the process of making a Ten-Year Plan. I suggest starting at the tenth year and listing what you would like to accomplish. This starting point helps establish your goals and becomes the seed of your plan to change and take charge of your life.

Here are some examples: be licensed in your occupation, (CPA, Nurse, Architect, Human Resource, Engineer), have a good paying job, house paid for, bachelor's or masters degree, save one hundred thousand dollars (many times the bulk of savings are in the latter years of the plan), travel, new vehicle of choice, married, family. You may want to be self-employed. If so, there will need to be a business plan worked into the Ten-Year Plan.

Now that we have some things to work with, we can begin distributing them throughout the years. This will help decide what you need to do first to begin to prioritize. During the first year is where most of the research will take place. It is your starting point and some things may have to be adjusted.

Everyone's plan will be different. The following is just an example. You can always add or remove certain wants and desires until the plan is where you want it and where it will work for you. Every year add another year so you always have a Ten-Year Plan in operation.

Year One:
    (most of these happen in the first few months)
    Start making the Ten-Year plan.
    Check into school,
        get details, classes needed, start times.
    Contact headhunter (employment agency)
        for better job in chosen occupation.
    Update resume.
    Evaluate how expenses can be cut.
    Obtain information for occupation license test.
    Begin a daily study program for test.
    Take test.
    Start school during this year if at all possible.
    Begin emergency fund.

In year two is where you get deeper into making your plan become more realistic. Here is where you start making it all happen. This is the year you start a savings plan, possibly a thousand dollars per month or even a hundred dollars per month. Save whatever you can realistically afford after dropping all of the extraneous extras. They can be added back into your lifestyle at a later date.

Be sure the savings amount coincides with the target amount in your plan. It is not uncommon to be unable to save very much until about the fourth or fifth year. However, in the first year you need to immediately begin saving an emergency fund. In the beginning, there's not much room for fun stuff. Taking charge of your life must become the fun stuff.

In the second year you begin making an extra payment on the house. You take that occupational license test. You continue your schooling, studying, and taking care of the necessities. School may take less time, depending on the program, so make adjustments in your outline. You may notice at this time it requires you to do some delegating, even though things may not be done to your standards.

Year Two:
    Start savings.

    Extra payment on the house.

    Take occupational license test
        (if not already done so).

    Add to emergency fund.

    Continue school.

    Update resume.

Year Three:
    Make every effort
        to make two extra house payments this year.

    Continue going to school.

    Try your best to save at least five hundred dollars
        more than last year, or more if possible.

    Update resume.

Year Four:
    Three extra house payments.

    If not yet working in chosen occupation,
        continue applying for jobs.

    Update resume.

    Still saving all possible monies.

    Continue school.

Year Five:
>Get employment in your field of study (if not already done so).
>Increase house payments to four.
>Take a short vacation but keep within budget.
>Continue those extra house payments.
>Make adjustments to plan
>>according to income and timetable.
>
>Graduate from school.

Year Six:
>If in a relationship
>>start thinking about marriage and family.
>
>Continue extra house payments.
>Increase savings accordingly.
>Make realistic adjustments to plan.
>Possibly purchase new vehicle.

Year Seven:
>Continue extra house payments;
>>make adjustments to achieve goal.
>
>Make travel plans.
>Add new desires to plan.
>Double or triple up on savings;
>>make adjustments to achieve saving goal.

Year Eight:
> By this time most of the
>> Ten-Year Plan has been accomplished.
>
> Continue savings.
>
> Continue extra house payments.
>
> Make plans to accomplish things you've added to
>> the next years of your plan.

Year Nine:
> Extra house payments; make adjustments
>> in payment to achieve goal.
>
> Continue saving.
>
> Continue plans and adjustments for future events.
>
> Continue travel.

Year Ten:
> During this year complete Ten-Year Plan
>
> If house is not paid, make adjustments
>> and set new target date; continue with extra payments.
>
> Continue savings plan.
>
> Continue with details for future events.
>
> By this time, you have created a
>> new you with positive habits and behaviors.
>
> Continue traveling, should you choose.

The Life Coach's client's plan may be simpler than this example Ten-Year Plan or it may be more complicated. Keep in mind you will always have a Ten Year Plan in process. The objective here is to make a plan detailed enough to keep the client on track. I suggest meditation regularly to avoid the many pitfalls he will encounter, especially in the beginning while the changes are becoming the new norm.

It has been my experience that having and working a Ten-Year Plan can give Purpose and works wonders in neutralizing depression, plus many other emotional issues. This is especially true when Consistency of Purpose is kept in the forefront of your mind. There are tools to help you stay focused and on track.

(Refer to Motivation and Focus, Meditation, Purpose)

Public, Private, Secret Self

This tool helps the client separate his behaviors, thoughts, and beliefs into categories. We will be working on the premise that within all of us there is a Public Self, a Private Self, and a Secret Self. It is important to differentiate between each one and to know when to display each particular behavior.

The Public Self is that part which we reveal in the workplace. This part is also expressed at social events, when meeting someone for the first time, and any time when attending to public affairs and taking care of business. Here is where social norms are displayed in public.

The Private Self is that part shared with family and friends. People get to know us on a more personal level. They learn

Public, Private, Secret Self

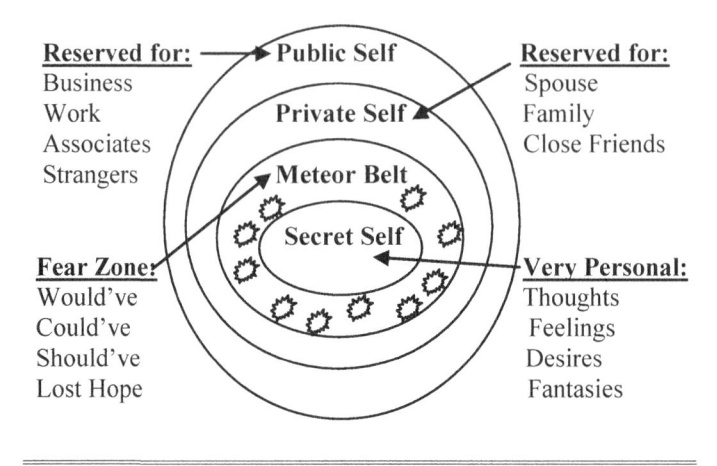

Reserved for: → Public Self
Business
Work
Associates
Strangers

Private Self
Meteor Belt
Secret Self

Reserved for:
Spouse
Family
Close Friends

Fear Zone:
Would've
Could've
Should've
Lost Hope

Very Personal:
Thoughts
Feelings
Desires
Fantasies

The **Public Self** is that part which we reveal in the workplace. The **Private Self** is that part shared with family and friends. The **Fear Zone (Meteor Belt)** is all of the rules, beliefs and social norms we encounter that keep us from our **Secret Self**. The **Secret Self** is unique because it is that part usually outside of the social norm which we may fear to express because of ridicule or being ostracized.

about our temperament, idiosyncrasies and quirks. They also learn something about our personal experiences, and how we handle or cope with them. This is the part displayed when we are relaxing and just being our-self.

The Secret Self is unique because few people are aware that this part of self exists. It is as though they are in denial of it or they simply repress the feelings and behaviors that are

264

contained within the Secret Self. It is that part outside of the social norm which we may fear to express because of ridicule or being ostracized.

This part is guarded by what I call a meteor belt of would've, could've, should've, ought to', do's, and don'ts which guards from that part we deem as unacceptable. It also can be something that you accept about yourself on a very private level but which you may experience in utmost secrecy.

This meteor belt protects most from admitting to themselves that those feelings and urges ever surface in their thoughts. Denial of Secret Self is denying an important aspect of self. Accepting the Secret Self doesn't mean it needs to be acted upon, for various reasons. It simply means you accept and embrace all of yourself.

The Life Coach may point out to his client the importance of exploring all aspects of self. Over the years, on several occasions, I have been told by clients they have feelings of guilt and don't know why. Some have said they have crazy thoughts about things that they are ashamed to mention.

My response has been: "the only way I know of dealing with those feelings of guilt and 'crazy thoughts' is to bring them to the surface so they can be addressed." I always reassure my clients that I do not judge, and what is talked about stays with me unless he chooses to say something to someone else.

Many times feelings of guilt and/or feelings of not being good enough are so elusive the client can't put their finger on the cause. I will usually do hypnosis with them, and use a metaphor to help them understand and change those feelings.

Also, during the hypnosis session, I will give a series of post-hypnotic suggestions. I will suggest they become aware on a conscious level of all those repressed thoughts and feelings, suggesting those thoughts and feelings can be reframed to bring balance into their life. This process may take many sessions and the use of several tools.

Mind Levels

The Mind Levels Tool involves the concept that certain things within us take place on different levels in our subconscious mind. This tool is just a way of helping the client understand how to make corrections in the way he thinks, feels, and behaves. These corrections will alter his perception.

(Refer to Reframing)

It is a theory which has helped me explain to my clients the pitfalls they may encounter on their journey to self-discovery. Of course, we are, All-Encompassing, Multidimensional, and Omni-directional beings. However, the Mind Levels tool is an excellent way to simplify and explain a very complex topic. It is simply a tool I use and is not taken as a scientific study.

Life Coaching is much more than giving advice. It is a process of instructing and directing or guiding someone in the direction which they have chosen. When someone comes to seek my assistance, I view it as a private class about them and their life.

This class comes with homework and commitment on both parties. The tools I use to help them achieve their desired outcome were gathered and developed over many years, working with a variety of issues. The Mind Levels tool is one of my First Responders because it gives the client a visual or concept of how we will be approaching the changes he will be making.

When using this tool, I will begin with the following phrase. "Once upon a time in a land far, far away human beings came on the scene." I then continue explaining the Mind Level tool. I use a little humor off and on to help relieve the tension because, by this time we are talking about some pretty deep stuff.

When humans came on the scene they had a Conscious, a Subconscious, and an Autonomic Nervous System. They also developed a Critical Faculty which helped guard against injury to the belief system and to the organism as well. The Critical Faculty is part conscious and part subconscious, which will be discussed later in this chapter. I have heard some people refer to the Autonomic Nervous System as the unconscious mind.

Let's begin with the conscious mind. On a conscious level you don't even know your name. If you did, you would have to walk around saying my name is so and so (say your name), so your name and all the other pertinent information lie just below your level of awareness and are readily accessible.

In this theory of the mind, the conscious level is an intake channel. Its intakes includes olfactory (smell), kinesthetic (touch), visual (sight), auditory (sound), and palate (taste), just as it is presented. As information is taken in, it is altered by the perception of the individual in his subconscious.

The subconscious records what we learn and stores it in our Belief System. Although unintentional as it may be, I believe we are told at least twenty-five negatives for every

Mind Levels

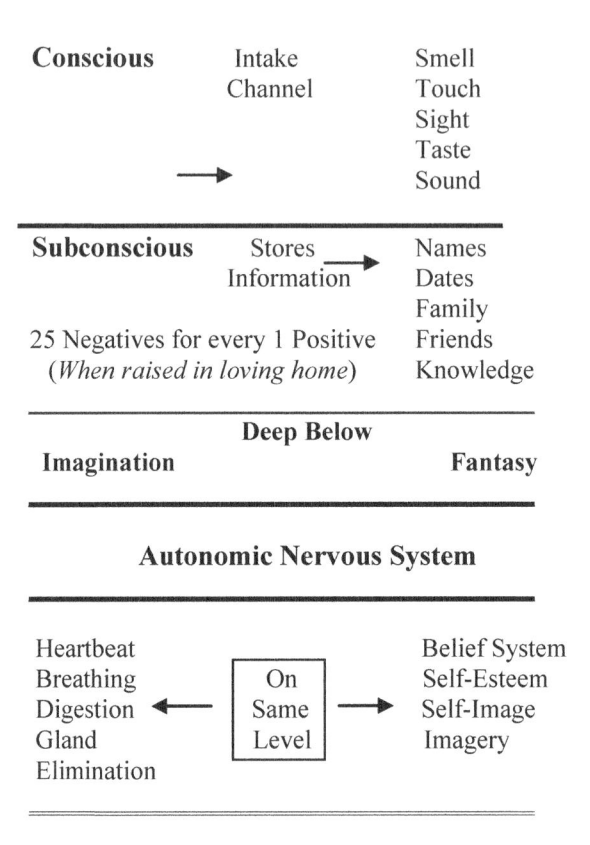

Conscious   Intake   Smell
                    Channel   Touch
                                    Sight
                                    Taste
          ⟶   Sound

Subconscious   Stores ⟶   Names
                    Information   Dates
                                    Family
25 Negatives for every 1 Positive   Friends
(When raised in loving home)   Knowledge

Deep Below

Imagination   **Fantasy**

===

Autonomic Nervous System

===

Heartbeat   Belief System
Breathing   ┌──────┐   Self-Esteem
Digestion   ⟵   │ On   │   ⟶   Self-Image
Gland   │ Same │   Imagery
Elimination   │ Level│
                   └──────┘

The illustration is to demonstrate why it's difficult to make changes in behavior. It is to give an example and explain the "depth" of the belief system, self-esteem, self-image, and the ability to use Imagery to see one's self differently.

one positive when raised in a loving home. These positives and negatives may be verbal and/or nonverbal. They also may be inferred by the way we perceive how we were treated.

If the individual had been abused mentally, physically, sexually or neglected in any way, then the twenty-five to one goes out the window. The perception of the individual could change that number, for example to twenty-five hundred to one, more or less. How he internalizes his experience is totally up to the individual and his perceptions.

We now move "deeper" into the subconscious in an attempt to help the client understand why it is so hard to make changes on his own. I explain "down" below imagination and fantasy is the Autonomic Nervous System. This level is out of control of the conscious mind.

We will want to keep in mind that imagination is a creation of the mind. It is a creative ability to form a mental image of something not present to the senses or not previously known or experienced. Imagination will play a major role in the journey into self while reframing negative experiences.

Fantasy is Imagination in action. To imagine something and then put it into action in your mind can be a very powerful experience. During my hypnosis scripts I will suggest the client imagine what it is like making certain changes. I then suggest he put himself into the situation and become the person who has made the changes and experience what it is like to be that person.

Here the Life Coach must use his own creativity and be sure to paint a very detailed picture in the client's mind. You will want to hallucinate the client's senses to help him imagine and then fantasize what it's like to become the person he wants to become.

Following is an example of a metaphor of how words can affect even the glands of the body. I tell of a friend who got married and moved to Point Loma in San Diego. He did not have to work any longer so he spent his time tending to his small lemon grove of about twenty-five to thirty trees.

Every time I came to visit, and shortly after the formalities with the wife and kids, he would usher me out into his lemon grove. Since I have a degree in horticulture, it was brain picking time. He had his trees named and numbered as well as notes about trimming and any special fertilizer he may have used.

I would make suggestions about how to open up (trim) certain trees. We would discuss how he could get more fruit and possibly make some of the sour lemons sweeter. While we were walking and talking, I would be squeezing and rolling a lemon in my hands that I got from the tree just outside his back door.

By the way, the lemons from this tree are the sourest lemons I have ever tasted. They were so sour they would almost give me lockjaw, and I like very sour lemons. At some point when were facing each other, I would bite into the lemon and the juice would squirt everywhere.

He would make a face and ask, "How in the world can you stand to eat that sour thing." I would usually respond by saying, "you are right. These are about the sourest lemons I have ever tasted." At this point, it felt like every gland in my body was reacting to how sour that lemon tasted.

I then ask my client if my talking about the sour lemons made his mouth water. Usually by the time I am halfway through the story, they are already making a face. I tell them, "This is hypnosis. I just affected the glands in your body with words and you are a grown adult. Can you imagine how words could affect a child who is defenseless?"

To continue painting a clear detailed picture in the client's mind, and after a quick explanation of imagination and fantasy, I explain what takes place in the Autonomic Nervous System as it applies to him making changes in his life. On this "level" is where things like the pupils dilating, breathing, digestion, and elimination take place.

As I write this information on the board, I begin explaining that on this same level are his belief system, self-esteem, self-image, and imagery. This is why it is so hard to make serious life changes and get to the root of a problem. Making changes requires making adjustments to the belief system.

The Belief System is what he has come to believe about himself. These beliefs are an accumulation of other people's wants, needs, desires, and beliefs, whether they have worked for those people or not. These people include parents, teachers, clergy, and any authority figures that were involved in the client's life.

Self-Esteem is how he feels about himself. Much of this comes from his beliefs and the way he has been treated by others, both directly and indirectly. Something as simple as being raised in a family of introverts can cause an extrovert to have self-esteem issues and vice versa. This can also include being right-brained in a left-brained family.

Self-Image is how one sees himself. It begins forming early in childhood and if it becomes negative, then problems are created and can show early in adolescence and continue on into adulthood. I have found a poor self-image can also be at the root of many behavioral problems.

Imagery is where the work takes place. The Life Coach uses this aspect to help the client create the person he has chosen to become. As the client is led through the process of reframing negative past experiences, he will begin to see himself differently. Imagery is where The Life Coach, with his words and metaphors, paints new images into the client's subconscious, just like the story about the lemons.

Now, the Critical Faculty comes into play. Although this aspect can help guard against harm both to the physical being and one's beliefs, it can also work against the individual's best interests. It also can keep us stuck in a way of believing that may cause us great emotional grief.

The Critical Faculty is part conscious and part subconscious. The major part of this aspect of the mind is subconscious. It is much like a submarine with its periscope above water watching for danger or threat while the submarine itself remains below water ready to take action.

Another way of saying this is much like the old saying "buyer beware," so you must stay on guard, you buy it, you own it, so stay on guard there is no warranty, you buy it, as is, no matter what you are told by the seller. This attitude can cause a person to throw out important information in order to protect oneself, just in case.

For example, if I say anything that is in direct opposition to your beliefs, you immediately throw it out as nonsense. Unfortunately, this can keep one stuck in a belief system that is not working in their best interests. The same goes for physical harm. If I suggest anything that may bring physical harm, it is also immediately thrown out in order to protect self.

This Critical Faculty must be bypassed in order to make changes to the belief system. As an example, I will ask my clients if they would walk barefoot on two thousand degree coals. Nearly every time they laugh and say, "No, not a chance."

I respond and say, "What if I walk across the coals with a million dollars in my hand and offer it to you if you will walk across the coals with me?" Some of them take me up on the offer. In their case, I just bypassed their Critical Faculty. Others refuse my offer of the million dollars, so I will make them another offer.

I will use information about their family or something near and dear to their heart. As an example, I will say, "What if I could prove to you that your family would stay well and healthy for the rest of their lives, would you walk with me?" As soon as they say "yes," then I just bypassed their Critical Faculty. Thus far, I've had no one turn me down on the latter example.

The Life Coach must have a plan of his intentions. Working with the Mind Levels Tool is a good starting point with new clients. This is especially true for those who have little to no knowledge as to how they became and remain stuck in a Belief System that seems to be working against them. At first, it can be very scary for someone to tamper with what they have come to believe.

Other Products

By Dr. Rondall L. Bailes, CHD

The Art & Structure of Metaphor In Hypnosis

This Hypnosis Text Book illustrates how to structure effective metaphors. It covers the details involved and shows several examples and explanations of metaphors.

For more information on the use and structure of metaphors, refer to The Art & Structure of Metaphor In Hypnosis, by: Dr. Rondall Bailes DCH. It can be ordered by hard copy or down loaded from my website.

www.peoplereadingbodylanguage.com

People Reading: Easy To Use Methods & Techniques

A five-disc DVD video course on how to ready body language, gestures and gesture clusters. These principals are explained through demonstrations and illustrations.

Disc 1 – First Impressions

Learn the meaning of the Handshake, Skin and Hair Texture, Eye Movements, Angle of the Feet and How to Speak to someone below their level of awareness.

Disc 2 – Facial Profiles

Covers the Different Types of Facial Profiles and how to read people by utilizing these Inherited Traits.

Disc 3 – Gestures

Teaches the meaning of many simple gestures. The subconscious body movements will give you insight into the strengths and weaknesses of individuals.

Disc 4 – Social Gesture Clusters

Gives you the valuable advantage into how to interpret several Gestures into a Cluster for a quick reading of someone's state of mind and overall attitude in a Social Setting.

Disc 5 – Business Gesture Clusters

Helps you become aware of the many Power Plays which often occur in the Business Environment. Why are your treated the way you are? Positive or Negative.

Dream Journey – DVD

The Dream Journey DVD teaches how to work dreams and interpret their meaning. Each individual has their own unique dream language. Through the process of asking the correct questions the individual is led to the deep meaning of their dreams, by understanding what the pictures and images streaming from their subconscious, means to them. This process is demonstrated through illustrations and also reveals the series of questions that need to be asked for them to interpret their own dreams.

Available for download or hard copy at:
www.peoplereadingbodylanguage.com

Coming Soon

Life Coach Manual
Developmental Tools
Volume Two

In this dynamic book, I discuss several of the developmental processes/tools I have developed and used with my clients in my Hypnosis and Life Coach Practice over the past thirty years.

In this Life Coach Manual, illustrations and explanations are used to help the client understand how to take the next step on his journey to self-discovery. These tools are more complex than the First Responder Tools, Volume One of the Life Coach Manual.

The tools outlined in this volume of the Life Coach Manual illustrate how to identify and resolve deep issues so the client may experience a meaningful inner-peace. These integral tools and techniques assist the Life Coach in helping his client understand many aspects of his personality, and thinking style. It also illustrates how those aspects interact within his self.

Guided Meditation Series

Many of the series of metaphors I have used over the years to help relieve stress and tension including the areas of pre- and post-surgery, coping with cancer, grief, relationship issues as well as other topics.

www.peoplereadingbodylanguage.com